ESCAPE FROM
BROADMOOR

THE TRIALS AND STRANGULATIONS OF
JOHN THOMAS STRAFFEN

GORDON LOWE

The
History
Press

For Anne, Amelia and Verity

Front cover image: © Getty Images

First published 2013

The History Press
The Mill, Brimscombe Port
Stroud, Gloucestershire, GL5 2QG
www.thehistorypress.co.uk

© Gordon Lowe, 2013

The right of Gordon Lowe to be identified as the Author
of this work has been asserted in accordance with the
Copyrights, Designs and Patents Act 1988.

British Library Cataloguing in Publication Data.
A catalogue record for this book is available from the British Library.

ISBN 978 0 7524 8988 9

Typesetting and origination by The History Press
Printed in Great Britain
Manufacturing managed by Jellyfish Solutions Ltd

My mother said, I never should
Play with the gypsies in the wood.
If I did, she would say,
'Naughty little girl to disobey.'
The wood was dark, the grass was green,
In came Johnny with a tambourine.

Nursery Rhyme

LIST OF ILLUSTRATIONS

Diagram used in the trial of Straffen's route from Broadmoor to Farley Hill. *Trial of JT Straffen (Fairfield and Fullbrook)*

Trial Plan of Farley Hill village. *Trial of JT Straffen (Fairfield and Fullbrook)*

Front Page *Daily Mirror* 1 May 1952.

Churchill's Minute 8 June 1952. *The National Archives*

Churchill's Minute 5 September 1952. *The National Archives*

Home Secretary's Reply to Churchill, page 1 of 2, 8 September 1952. *The National Archives*

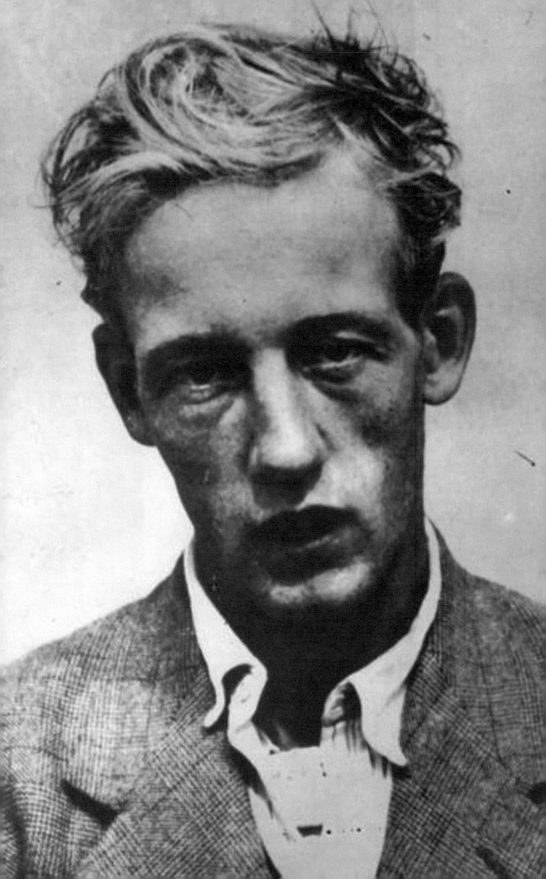

1

I f John Thomas Straffen had not escaped from Broadmoor Institution on 29 April 1952, then the day might have been remembered for its beautiful weather. For the first time that year the residents in the village of Crowthorne, at the bottom of the hill from Broadmoor's twenty foot-high redbrick walls, were opening their windows and back doors to air their houses and hear the birds singing outside, while others decided to risk afternoon tea in the garden under a warm sun and blue sky. Daffodils were out on the lawns and primroses grew in clusters on the banks of country lanes. The woods were full of bluebells and children were coming out of school to play on their bikes in the streets. Spring breeds expectancy, but no one could have expected what was in store that afternoon.

Mrs Spencer in Crowthorne was telephoning through an order for dog food and had been promised delivery in the afternoon; seven miles away Mrs Sims in the village of Farley Hill was busying herself setting out a tray of tea things in anticipation of her sister-in-law arriving; and Mrs Loyalty Kenyon in Farley Hill House was halfway through her regular afternoon rest, safe in the knowledge that her two children were in the capable hands of their German nanny; the three of them were already playing a game of hide and seek in the garden among the shrubs and trees bordering the lawn. Mrs Miles in Wokingham was getting the car out of the garage to make a trip into Farley Hill to collect clothes for the Women's Institute. Mr Taylor was starting his afternoon in the office, worried whether the local cricket pitch needed watering; he decided to make an inspection first thing after work. Mr Sims, who was working on an estate near Farley Hill, had warned his wife he would be half-an-hour late back after work because he was going to deliver a load of wood to his father, so there was a chance he'd miss tea with her and his sister at Pillar Box Cottage.

Linda Bowyer, aged 5, in her school on Farley Hill high street, could hardly wait for school to be over to get on her bike with the other children. She knew it was a good day because they'd been let out into the school playground during the dinner hour and this hadn't been possible for ages because of the weather. Even though Broadmoor Institution was seven miles away, east of Farley Hill, she still knew it by name. The other children called it a loony bin, and she called it a loony bin, but she didn't really know what that meant. It was a place you put mad people, she knew that much, and so she thought it must be a bin for mad people.

But a black cloud was about to cast its shadow over all of them – and for one it would shut out the sun forever.

The black cloud was John Thomas Straffen. At that moment he was lying spreadeagled over the slate roof of an outbuilding behind the main wall of Broadmoor. His thick-soled working boots had slipped as he groped his way up the roof. As he found his feet, the door of the main building behind opened. He prayed it wasn't Mr Cash, the work party attendant, but it was John's co-patient Whitcombe.

'Mr Cash wants to know when you're coming back in?' Whitcombe shouted loud enough for Mr Cash to hear inside the building. He couldn't stop himself smiling at the sight of John in three layers of clothing slipping and sliding around the roof like a beached whale.

'Tell him I'm shaking my duster,' John shouted back. 'Back in a jiff.'

Whitcombe shut the door with a bang. John continued his ascent and clutched the top of the wall, levering himself onto the top to take a nervous peek over the side. He blinked at the road winding down the hill that he had last seen from the back of the police car which brought him into Broadmoor six months ago.

Like a passenger contemplating jumping over the ship's side, common sense told him to give up and go back down the roof. It looked an awful long way down. What John had shouted back to Whitcombe just then was the truth. He was shaking his duster, or had been until he jumped onto the disinfectant drums under the wall and hauled himself onto the shed roof – but he'd never be back.

He'd never be back because if you escaped from Broadmoor they didn't send you back. He told everyone that but no one knew where he'd got it from. He wanted to escape to show them he could be free and not harm anyone. That would show them he hadn't done the two Bath murders. They'd say, 'Look, he got out of the place and didn't hurt a fly.'

He looked over the edge of the wall again and saw a fire hydrant cover that might break his fall. Then again, it might break his legs, he didn't know whether to aim for that or the grass bank.

John swung off the top of the wall, clutching the stone ledge with his hands and allowing his feet to dangle under him in space. Then he closed his eyes and let go.

2

ight months previously, at 2.30 p.m. on the afternoon of Sunday 15 July 1951, John Straffen left his family home in their crowded flat in Bath to make his weekly visit to the cinema. But instead of following his usual route across the city to the Forum Cinema, he turned in the opposite direction up Lansdown Road towards Camden Crescent. He was dressed in a striped blue suit with an open necked, white shirt and made light work of the climb up the steep hill, moving with a long, gangling stride, mouth slack and eyes fixed on the pavement ahead, without any attempt to look at or acknowledge the couples and families making their way to Victoria Park or Parade Gardens to cool off on the hot afternoon.

John enjoyed his Sundays. It was a day off from the labours of the market garden just outside the city in Bathampton where he'd worked steadily for the last few weeks, a day when he could get up late, have a good roast lunch cooked by his mother – her best meal of the week – and then the afternoon on his own at the matinée performance of whatever was on at the cinema. It didn't really matter what the film was, but he preferred a good adventure like a western or Robin Hood, and that meant usually the Forum or Odeon cinemas, the two largest cinemas in Bath almost facing each other across Southgate Street. In fact they were so near each other that if the queue to get in looked too long at one, then he would simply cross the street to join the other, whatever the film.

Sometimes he'd see one film at the Forum and then watch the other at the Odeon, even if the programme had already started or was in the middle of the supporting film. They knew him at both cinemas and had stopped trying to work out what he wanted. He was such a frequent customer the usherettes during the intervals would let him have an ice-cream even if he'd forgotten his money.

But this Sunday hadn't gone well. John hadn't felt like getting up and his mother had said that until he was up, with his bed made, he wouldn't get any lunch or be allowed out to the cinema. He said she could keep her lunch, but she knew he didn't mean it because he wouldn't miss Sunday lunch for anything. But not going to the pictures – that was different. This was his Sunday afternoon and now he was 21 she couldn't stop him. So he got up and made his bed, muttering and cursing, but not too loud in case his father heard and gave him a beating.

What John did was to leave the flat at 2 p.m. as usual and walk out into the Paragon but, instead of crossing the road and going down Broad Street towards the cinemas, he made a sharp right in the opposite direction up Lansdown, and sped up a bit so that no one from the flat would see him.

He had friends up the hill on Lansdown he could meet and moan to about being told to make his bed, friends who understood this and saw it wasn't fair.

And there was another thing that wasn't fair. Last week he'd been seen by the doctor who had to assess him now he was 21 and still on licence from the offenders' institute. The doctor said he could stay at home and get on with his job but they'd have to keep an eye on him and reassess him. So if he did anything stupid then the police could put him back inside and that wasn't fair.

It was always the police – they were out to get him even when he did things right.

The friends he could have a bit of a moan at lived behind Camden Crescent among the trees in a den they called The Private. No one knew about The Private – not even his mother, it was that secret. He'd never told her or anyone about The Private.

There were a couple of children playing outside Belvedere halfway up Lansdown, but when he stopped to smile at them, they stuck their tongues out at him and said rude things. Anyway, he didn't know them and they didn't seem very nice.

People shouldn't be rude to him, that wasn't very nice either. At the Hortham Colony, the institute near Bristol where he'd been sent for pinching things, they'd told him what to do. The police who put him in there told him what to do. He hadn't always made his bed at Hortham and Mr Beaver had thrown his weight around telling him what to do and said he wouldn't have lunch unless he made his bed. Now his mother was acting like Mr Beaver.

A couple of hundred yards up from Belvedere he turned right into Camden Crescent, one of Bath's half-moon Regency crescents and, head down and mouth open, he forked left to walk behind the crescent towards The Private.

Suddenly he wasn't alone. A girl was stooped over the grass to the left of the path, picking something out of the grass.

John stopped. He said hello and smiled at her. She smiled back, not like the rude ones outside Belvedere. 'What are you doing?' he asked.

'Picking flowers,' she replied, and stuck out a small bunch of white flowers to show him.

'What's your name?' he asked.

'Brenda,' she said, and went on picking flowers.

'Are you allowed to pick the flowers, Brenda?' asked John.

'They're wild,' she said.

Then she ignored him and he wondered if he was being rude. 'Do you have to make your bed?' he asked.

When this didn't produce an answer he said, 'I can show you where there's better flowers higher up, if you like.'

At this she looked up, more interested, and nodded. She was so nice he could see people might be upset if anything happened to her, especially the police. He took her by the hand and walked along to the copse. Nobody had seen them and nobody told them to stop. At the copse he lifted her over the wall and climbed over himself.

'Where are the flowers?' she asked.

'I'll show you,' he said and they walked along under the high wall at the back of the copse, where the flowers grew in a white carpet under the trees.

The girl started to pick them, and as she did so he bent down behind her, wrapped his fingers around her neck and squeezed until she flopped and didn't move. She didn't make any noise, and he'd expected her to make some sort of noise. So he took her by the shoulders and banged her head on a stone at the foot of the wall to make sure. Then leaving her exactly where she fell, he jumped back over the wall and started walking down the back of Camden Crescent.

As he passed the spot where he'd met the girl he looked at his watch and decided there was still time to get to the film. Back in the street he paused a moment to take out his handkerchief and brush off some of the burrs and pollen that had stuck to his trousers, before taking the long route up to Lansdown Crescent and then down into Bath.

He was a bit early for the film and sat near the front with an ice-cream. There was no one else much around in the 1/6 rows at the front. He thought about how long it would take the police to find the girl and how long it would take them to try to find who did it. He'd waste their time now instead of them wasting his.

All in all it hadn't been a bad Sunday. He'd got his lunch and he'd get the film.

The title of the feature film that afternoon was *Shockproof*.

3

Mrs Doris Pullen looked out of her window in the basement flat at 1 Camden Crescent at just after 2 p.m. that Sunday afternoon for her daughter, expecting to see her playing in the garden. Brenda was usually out there with her dolls in the pram, but sometimes she'd play at the back of the garden beside Rough Lane. Anyway, she'd have to come back in soon because it was Sunday school at 3 p.m. down at Hay Hill and she'd have to start getting ready.

Today had been a normal Sunday for the Pullen family. Doris and her husband Alf had taken Brenda down to the eleven o'clock service at Christ Church, Julian Road, and sat near the back like they always did. Alf had only been demobbed from the army for a couple of years and didn't hold much with church or anything to do with religion. 'Men in frocks' he called the clergy, and if there was a God why did He let them do all those awful things in the war. Doris said that might or might not be the case but they had a duty to Brenda to bring her up properly, and that included church on Sunday morning and Sunday school in the afternoon. Christ Church was Brenda's infants' school round the back of the church and it wouldn't look good if they didn't show up on Sundays. When Brenda was old enough – she was only six now – then she could decide for herself.

Brenda was not their real daughter. They were her foster parents while her widowed mother Connie Goddard lived and worked at the Hospital for Rheumatic Diseases in Bath. But they loved Brenda as if she was their own. She was a lovely girl, with sandy hair tied up in ribbons in long ringlets; she could play by herself for hours with her dolls and prams. They knew her at the hospital as well when she came in and out to visit her mother. Although the family kept to themselves, the neighbours knew Brenda by sight playing in the house or garden.

If Brenda did play outside the garden in Rough Lane, it would be with her friend Ruth, but neither of them went up to the copse, known locally as The Private, further along the back of the crescent. For children of Brenda's age, The Private looked like a fairy castle up on the hill, surrounded by a high wall and full of secrets among the thick foliage and trees enjoyed by the older and tougher children.

Mrs Pullen now went out into the garden, looked and then called over the wall, but she still couldn't see Brenda. She called but couldn't hear her. They had a rule that Brenda didn't wander far from the garden gate onto Rough Lane unless she was with Ruth and then they could play together in the grass above the lane. It was safe enough from the road at the front of the crescent, and one of the reasons the Pullens had rented the flat was to give Brenda somewhere secure to play.

Next she went back into the house to check Brenda hadn't somehow gone in to see Alf, which was unlikely as he invariably went to sleep after Sunday lunch and a cup of tea, thankful not to be involved with Sunday school. When Brenda wasn't there either her stomach started to knot. She instinctively knew something was wrong; Brenda just wasn't the sort of girl to go off on her own.

Mrs Pullen woke her husband and walked back to the rear of the garden, while he went out into the front of Camden Crescent to look there. Even now she didn't think of going up to the copse to look. She didn't really know anything about The Private; Brenda had never mentioned it, and the copse didn't start until a long way down the crescent at No. 14 anyway. It was eerily quiet now at the back, with all the children who might usually play there having their lunch or getting ready for Sunday school. It would have helped if there had been someone to ask, even if they hadn't seen Brenda.

But there was someone. As she walked back through the garden gate for a second time, praying that Alf might have found out something at the front, Mrs Pullen caught site of a man in a blue suit striding across the road in front of Camden Crescent. He bent down a moment to brush something off his trousers and then turned up Lansdown Road towards

St Stephen's Church. Striding was the wrong word, because he wasn't quite co-ordinated and he seemed to be looking down at the ground and running his hand through his fair hair. Then he turned the corner and was gone, as quickly as he'd appeared.

Up until three o'clock Mrs Pullen was as much concerned about Brenda missing Sunday school as anything else but, after calling on the neighbours, including Ruth and her parents, with no success they wasted no more time. Mr Pullen went out to the telephone box at 3.30 p.m. to ring the police.

By coincidence Detective Inspector Tom Coles, head of Bath CID, lived less than a stone's throw from The Private, his house facing the gate into the far end of the copse behind the crescent. He knew Brenda quite well, and was aware of her playing outside No. 1 as he walked into town. When he got the call from the central police station, Coles started organising a search party and soon had no less than fourteen CID officers on the job.

The copse was not at first their prime target. The Pullens were specific that Brenda did not play up there, and entry into the copse was difficult for a young child with its high walls and too far away for Brenda to reach in such a short time.

As the search widened, with some of the neighbours helping the police, it inevitably reached The Private. It wasn't so much the density of the trees and undergrowth that slowed the search, but the steep slope that made it hard to stand up at all.

It was DC Jim Drew, at about 6.30 p.m. in the evening, who found Brenda, at the foot of the wall between the back of No. 18 and St Stephen's Lane, about fifteen to twenty yards from the gate. There had been no effort to hide her, and some of the flowers she'd been picking were near her shoulder with the rest in a bunch under her arm.

4

John Straffen stretched his long legs under the cinema seat in front of him and let the film blot out the rest of the world. Up on the screen in *Shockproof* a parole officer was falling for his parolee, who'd taken the rap for a crime committed by her gambler lover. It was a good plot and he watched, chin up and mouth hanging open, until the lights went up and the usherettes were turfing them out. He walked home by Evans' fish shop near the abbey courtyard and bought himself fish and chips. Only when he'd eaten them did he remember the girl. They'd be looking for her – perhaps they'd found her already.

He'd cause a big nuisance, he knew that. But that was the idea, wasn't it? Whose fault was that? When they'd assessed him in Hortham Colony they should have given him a clean licence and he could have come home, and not have to worry about doing anything wrong or being sent back to Hortham where they told him what to do every minute of the day. When he was working on the farm he took that bag of walnuts and they sent him back to Hortham. Suppose he took something at the market garden now they might send him back to Hortham. Suppose someone framed him and they accused him of taking a plant or something?

Now they'd be so busy looking for the girl and who did it they wouldn't have time to worry about him.

He wasn't sorry. Anyone could see why he did it.

John wondered if his own probation officer, Mr Harding, had seen *Shockproof* and whether he had beautiful girls on his list and if he'd fallen in love with them. He would have to say so because that would be against the rules, falling for people on your list.

John finished the chips and threw the empty newspaper down on the pavement in disgust. He got a dirty look from some posh lady dressed up for evening service at Bath Abbey. He stood quietly in front of the abbey for a moment, looking at the angels climbing ladders to heaven up the front of the building, with the same look of wonder he wore in the cinema.

When he got home after a walk around the city, his mother gave him his usual supper of hot milk and bread with a sprinkle of sugar on the top. He liked to eat it at the kitchen table listening to the abbey bells ringing out one peel after another; he could imagine the angels going up and down their ladders singing the hymns they sang at Hortham. They might even stop the service in the abbey and ask if any member of the congregation knew anything about a murder up behind Camden Crescent, and if so would they please report to the police station.

They did that at Hortham when he escaped.

As he lay in bed that night, John smiled. He'd never take the rap for the girl. He knew that because they had no witnesses. Just a few days before there had been a murder of a girl in Windsor. It had been all over the *Daily Mirror*, the only paper he read. They had not caught the murderer, it said, although a number of people had been quizzed. Police from neighbouring forces had been brought in.

That'd given him the idea.

Before he fell asleep John thought what an easy way this was to waste police time – so easy he might even do it again.

5

After twenty-four hours the chief constable of Bath contacted the Flying Squad in London. It was not unusual in these circumstances to call in the boys from Scotland Yard, and it was not seen as a sign of weakness in a local force. Bath had the occasional domestic murder like any other city, especially with men coming back from the war and finding wives or girlfriends had been unfaithful or left them altogether, and these crimes could be sorted out in a few days by the local CID. But child murder was different. As was often the case with child murder there were no obvious clues as to who might have committed the crime. The only unusual features with this one were that no attempt had been made to hide the body and there had been no sexual interference.

On the morning of Tuesday 17 July Superintendent Rudkin and DS Foster arrived at Bath Spa station from London and were met by Tom Coles and the chief constable himself. Rudkin was a Bunter-like figure with a centre hair parting and a cigarette constantly in one hand. He looked more like a repertory actor than a detective, and the chief constable made a note that Rudkin and his colleague would need a good lunch. They were driven to the central police station and introduced to the local investigation team, given an update on progress – or lack of it – and then taken onto the Francis Hotel in Queen Square where rooms and a good lunch were booked for them.

Tom Coles watched them leave for their hotel and relaxed a little. They hadn't suggested anything very original, just to get samples of Brenda's clothing and the blood found on the stone behind her body off to the lab in Birmingham. They suggested it was someone local who knew the area judging by the difficulty the murderer must have had in getting them both over the wall into the copse and then selecting the spot for the murder. But then Tom felt he didn't need the Flying Squad to tell him all that.

For the second time that day Tom went through the list he'd put together in the last twenty-four hours of men with records of child interference. The list wasn't long and the offences weren't serious, mostly involving hanging around school gates and that sort of thing. Towards the bottom of the list was the name of John Thomas Straffen, and he was only on it because he'd threatened a girl four years ago when he was 17. Straffen's line was more petty pilfering and escaping from youth offenders' institutions. Tom had known him and his family for years, and was rather pleased that he seemed to be settling down these days into a job.

Over the following couple of days DC Smith was given the job of rounding up these individuals and bringing them into the station for interview, starting with the ones they knew weren't working and would be at home, and then making appointments to see the workers at a time that wouldn't clash with their jobs and raise unnecessary suspicions. John Straffen fell into this second category as he'd been working as a general labourer in a market garden for the last ten weeks or so, and DC Smith arranged with his mother to pick him up from the flat at 2 Fountain Buildings at the bottom of Lansdown hill. The request caused little stir in the Straffen household, a cramped flat that John shared with his parents, brother and three sisters at the top of a grand Georgian building owned by Bath City Council, because they'd grown almost immune to John's troubled history with the police through his boyhood and teenage years.

The first signs of future problems were John starting to speak late and then a speech defect that made him hard to understand. The family had returned to Bath after six years in India following John's father's discharge from the army. John, now 8, immediately started giving trouble and was referred to the child guidance clinic for pilfering and truanting. A year later it was the juvenile court for stealing a purse from a little girl and two years' probation. His probation officer found John impossible, not least because John didn't seem to understand what probation meant and at school couldn't grasp the difference between right and wrong.

Things were difficult for Mrs Straffen trying to bring up a family of five in cramped conditions at the top of a four-storey house, so it may not have come as a huge surprise to her when John's probation officer took him to see a psychiatrist, who classified him as a mental defective under the Education Act 1921.

Then the juvenile court sent him to a couple of residential homes for mental defectives, where he was found to be well behaved but nervous and timid, with two significant characteristics: he was always a solitary with no friends, and he took correction badly, going off to sulk by himself if ticked off.

Then, at 14, John strangled two prize geese belonging to an officer at the home. At 16, after being discharged from the homes, he started stealing from unoccupied houses. At 17 he assaulted and threatened a 13-year-old girl and six weeks after that he strangled five chickens belonging to the father of a girl with whom he'd had a quarrel. He left the bodies of the birds in the chicken house. But he was not charged for the chickens because he used the occasion to admit to other charges of housebreaking. Instead, he was certified again as a feeble-minded defective and sent to Hortham Colony at Bristol.

So it was on the evening of Friday 20 July 1951, at about 6 p.m. in the evening, that a weary DC Smith brought in a washed and scrubbed John Straffen to the small office occupied by Tom Coles at the police station in Orange Grove. The office looked over to the north side of Bath Abbey with its flying buttresses and acres of glittering windows that always brought Coles solace when things got tough at work. Sometimes in his lunch hour, when he got one, he'd walk over the street and quietly sit in a pew in the abbey to recharge.

Tom stood as the pair entered the office and stuck out a hand. 'Hello, John. How's tricks?'

'Not bad thank you, Mr Coles,' replied John.

'Take a pew then, lad,' said Tom, motioning to the chair in front of his desk. DC Smith went over to his desk and turned the chair to face their guest.

John Straffen sat with a straight back on the edge of his seat, his huge hands resting palm down on his knees. With his mouth open and set in a permanent grin, he looked straight across the desk at Tom Coles, his lips working slowly as if he was going to say something but didn't know how to say it. He wore a clean and pressed sports jacket over a white shirt. His cheeks were flushed, as if he had run up the stairs, and he only took a hand off his knee to push back the locks of hair flopping over his forehead.

'How's the job going, John?' asked Tom, at this stage making no effort to keep any written notes.

John's mouth worked for a second before answering. 'They got me on watering next week.'

'That's good. Boss treat you alright?'

'Keeps me busy,' replied John, and for the first time he looked over to DC Smith. 'Is anything the matter?'

'We haven't seen you for a bit, John, that's all,' said Tom. 'What d'you get up to at the weekends these days?'

John thought about this. 'I get Sundays off.'

Tom looked out of the window on his left. 'And do you do the things most people do on Sunday?'

'I go to the pictures in the afternoon, if that's what you mean.'

'Did you go to the pictures last Sunday, then?' asked Tom.

John looked down at his hands. 'I went to the Forum. I usually go to the Forum, unless it's no good, then I go to the Odeon,' he replied, closing his mouth for the first time.

'What film was that, then?'

John looked up at the ceiling. 'I don't know but I think it had shock in the title.'

'What time was that, John?'

John had to think carefully about this. 'About three thirty, I think.'

'Film any good?'

'Yes, it was good,' replied John.

Tom Coles looked back from the window and stuck both elbows on the desk to look John straight in the eyes. 'The thing is, lad, someone saw you on Sunday afternoon in Camden Crescent.'

It was a long shot because all Mrs Pullen had said was she saw a man, whom she described as about 35, in blue clothing, striding across the road outside the crescent. Tom waited for the reply, expecting John to explain again how he always went to the pictures.

Instead he said, 'Yes, that was me, I expect.'

Both officers blinked. 'What sort of time was that, John?' whispered Tom.

'Before I went to the pictures. I go for a walk sometimes before the pictures,' said John, starting to slur his words now the questions weren't so easy.

'What were you wearing – do you remember?'

'My suit.'

'Are you sure?'

'It was Sunday.'

'What colour's your suit?'

'Blue.'

'Are you sure?' Tom repeated.

'It's the only one I've got,' said John.

The two police officers sat back in their seats barely able to believe their luck. Straffen had been well down on their list and he was nearly fifteen years younger than the 35-year-old man described by Mrs Pullen. Tom lit up a cigarette and offered the packet to John.

'No thank you, Mr Coles, Mum doesn't allow it,' said John, pushing the packet back across the desk.

Tom took the opportunity to look at John's hands. They were big, but then he was a large man, six foot and strongly built. Their condition was probably what you'd expect of a man working as a labourer in a market garden: rough skinned – as he'd noticed when he shook hands when Straffen arrived – with warts or corns on the fingers where he had been pushing a barrow or wielding a shovel. The finger nails were black, which was surprising when the rest of him was so scrubbed. Tom saw that the flushed cheeks were permanent after being burnt over the last summer weeks working outside.

John found Tom studying him and looked back down to his knees, hanging his head to one side and allowing his mouth to hang slack again, his chin almost reaching his chest, like a small boy expecting to be ticked off.

'So, John,' continued Tom, 'as you went past Camden Crescent – that's the end near Lansdown Road – did you see anyone?'

John shook his head. 'No one in particular, I don't think.'

'Did you see a young girl playing in the grass there, for example?'

Tom pushed a photo of Brenda he'd been given by her parents over the desk towards John. She stood with her arms down by her side awkwardly held at attention, wearing what looked like her school dress with sensible black shoes. She smiled shyly from between ringlets of hair tied loosely in ribbons.

A car horn sounded outside in Orange Grove and John turned to look out of the window, distracted for a second. 'No young girl, just ordinary people as I remember, Mr Coles.'

'Not this young girl picking nice white flowers? She might have showed you the flowers?' persisted Tom, tapping his cigarette ash into an empty tobacco tin.

'No, I would have remembered that, Mr Coles. I don't have much to do with the children up there. They're a bit rude, as a matter of fact.'

'So you know the area, do you?'

John thought carefully about this. He'd had enough questioning from the police in his time to look out for trick questions. 'Only what I see on my walks,' he replied.

'Have you ever been up the back of the crescent, up Rough Hill as it's called?'

'No, nothing like that.'

'Along the back there to the wood, or The Private as it's known!'

'Never heard of it,' said John quickly.

Tom Coles made a second attempt to apply pressure. 'So what if I said someone had seen you up the back of Camden Crescent?'

John for the first time raised his voice and put his hands forward to grip the edge of the desk. 'Then I'd say they were lying, if they said that. I'd say it's a frame-up.'

Tom stubbed out his cigarette and sat back in his chair. He looked over to his colleague, who was writing all this down laboriously in a blue counsel's notebook. 'Make us a cup of tea, Smithie. No hurry, alright?'

This was code for DC Smith to stop the note taking, leave the room, and bring in the tea when asked.

Tom opened the drawer in his desk and produced a bag of toffees. 'Does your mum allow you to eat toffees, John?' he asked.

'She says they're bad for my teeth,' said John, but nevertheless he took one out of the bag and, with enough concentration to make him cross-eyed, pulled each end of the wrapper in his huge fingers and stuck the toffee into his mouth.

Tom Coles dealt with his toffee with less ceremony. 'The thing is, John, I recall about four years ago there was a bit of an upset when you threatened a girl. You said, "What would you do if I killed you? I've done it before." You remember that, don't you?'

John sucked his toffee and looked hard at the ceiling. 'I do remember that, Mr Coles.'

'You were 17 and she was 13 so we didn't do much about it, did we? You were both kids so we let it go. But maybe you had ideas about this little girl on Sunday, a little girl who couldn't put up much of a fight.'

'That girl when I was 17 hadn't been very nice to me.'

'Then six weeks later you strangled some chickens belonging to the father of another girl you fell out with. Maybe she wasn't nice to you either?'

John leaned forward in his seat and put his hands back on the table. 'I wasn't charged for that.'

'Only because you went on to tell us about the housebreaking. How many was it, thirteen cases of housebreaking?'

'Yes, but I told you about all that, Mr Coles.'

'Well, are you going to tell me about the girl this Sunday then, John?'

'Sunday I just went for a walk and to the pictures, like I told you. I don't want to go back to Hortham, so I wouldn't do anything like that.'

'This is a bit more serious than putting you back in Hortham Colony, John. You're a big boy now. The judge would have to make you an appointment with Mr Pierrepoint.'

John was about to take another toffee. 'Who's he?'

'He's the hangman, John.'

John's chin sunk to his chest, which rose and fell as his breathing became irregular. 'I don't like what you're saying, Mr Coles. That's all I'm saying,' said John and, keeping his head on his chest, he was true to his word and said nothing more.

Tom went into the corridor and gave DC Smith the nod for the tea and biscuits, but ten minutes and several biscuits later they hadn't got another word out of John Straffen. He sat drinking his tea noisily and crunching his biscuits, breaking each one and popping it into his half-open mouth.

'Tell you what, John,' said Tom at last, 'you write it all down for us if you don't want to talk about it, what you did that Sunday, and we'll leave you to finish your tea.' He put DC Smith's open notebook down in front of him on the desk with a pencil and left him to get on with it.

In the time it took the two police officers to smoke a couple of cigarettes, John filled a page with large, spidery writing describing in detail his walk, the visit to the pictures and the journey home, buying fish and chips on the way. He even drew a basic but accurate street map.

They couldn't charge him simply for being in the area at the time of the murder. Perhaps a chat with his employers might tell them some more. They watched him walk back into the evening down the station steps, loping along with ungainly strides, eyes fixed on the ground without interest in anyone else in the street.

'Well, Smithie,' said Tom, turning to his colleague, 'what do you think of our John Thomas Straffen?'

'Friendly enough, sir, like a child stuck in a grown-up body, I'd say – but it's when he looks at you with those blue eyes.'

'What about it?'

'He gives me the willies, if you know what I mean.'

He didn't say so, but Tom knew exactly what he meant.

6

All day Saturday Tom Coles mulled over what had been said during the interview. He seemed so preoccupied that his wife suggested they go out in the evening to give him a break from the investigation. He had reached the end of the list of possible suspects and the sight of the man 'in blue clothing' described by Mrs Pullen had led to John Straffen admitting he was there. But his explanation of having a Sunday walk before the cinema was quite plausible. He was a man of habit and a loner and this all helped him.

'Okay, we'll go to the flicks,' said Tom to his wife. 'But tomorrow afternoon, at the Forum.'

'What's on?' she asked.

'Doesn't matter, whatever's on.'

So on the Sunday afternoon they set off from their house down Camden Crescent. Tom held out the vague hope that they might even see John Straffen out on his Sunday walk striding along the crescent with that odd gait of his, but there was no sign of him as they turned down Lansdown Road. At the cinema they took up seats halfway back in the stalls, and looked around for the man who said he was always there on Sundays. Tom noticed groups of children congregating at the front, with a gap of a row of seats before the adults in the huge auditorium. Usherettes stood at the head of each aisle under dimmed houselights shining torches on their trays of ice-cream and sweets. A medley of tunes from the musicals blared out from behind the screen curtains.

Then, with about five minutes to go before the start of the show, a familiar figure dressed in a blue suit came loping down the aisle. He passed the adults without looking up, but then turned sharp right into the empty row of seats, sat down and produced a paper bag of sweets, which he proceeded to eat without looking up.

After the advertisements and Pathé news, the 'B' film featuring a Scotland Yard adventure lost the attention of the children in the front rows. Tom Coles looked over to John Straffen, whose face was now turned up to the vast screen, apparently so absorbed in the film he was forgetting to chew his sweets, his mouth open in an expression of wonder at the images flickering in front of him. Whenever the film reached a climax, usually someone getting shot or a car crashing in a chase, John would wave a hand in the air and look over to the children to join in with his excitement.

From time to time Tom would look again at this remote figure sitting on his own, in a no-man's-land between the adults and the children, not belonging to either or, as DC Smith had put it, a child living in an adult body.

Shockproof had been retained for a second week. Cornel Wilde, as the parole officer, again fell for his glamorous parolée serving a sentence for murder. There were no car chases and only one gunshot but John, clutching his bag of sweets, was rock still with concentration. Some of the children grew bored and left the cinema without even a glance from him.

After two hours the film ended abruptly and Tom Coles grabbed the arm of his wife. They were already halfway to the exit before the lights came up. Tom took a final glance over his shoulder to check they hadn't been seen, but the solitary figure was still in his seat, staring up at the screen as the curtains closed to end the show.

'Well,' asked Mrs Coles as they entered Southgate Street from the cinema, 'what does all that prove?'

'It proves our friend goes to the cinema on Sunday afternoon, nothing much else,' replied Tom.

'What does he do now?'

'If you believe his statement, he buys fish and chips and goes home.'

They walked through the abbey courtyard into Parade Gardens, where they stopped at the stone balustrade to watch couples below folding deckchairs on the lawns stretching down to the river. Players were packing their instruments on the bandstand for the journey home. 'Do you think your man has ever had a girlfriend?' Mrs Coles asked her husband.

'I shouldn't think so. I imagine women for him are like Patricia White in that film, glamorous, committing murder for the best of reasons without spilling a drop of blood. They come out of prison on parole after only five years and are given somewhere to live, with the men queueing up for them outside the door. The police are given a wild goose chase across the country, only to have the next one she tries to shoot forgive her from his hospital bed,' said Tom. 'Sad thing is, if any woman blinked at John Straffen he'd run a mile.'

On Monday morning DC Smith arrived in the office to find his boss at a clear desk staring into space. 'Don't take your coat off, Smithie. We're going gardening,' announced Tom Coles.

Tom had returned home with his wife on the previous evening from the film aware that he hadn't any evidence to pin this murder on John Straffen, except for the fact that he was in the immediate area on the afternoon of the murder. His family probably couldn't add very much. The mother had her hands full with a large family to look after, and there wouldn't be blood or much in the way of forensics to find on John's clothes. If it was John Straffen, then the whole abduction and murder would had to have happened in the few minutes from when Brenda went out to play to when Mrs Pullen saw the man in blue in the street outside.

But there was a person who might throw some light on all this, and that was John's employer out at the market garden where John had been working for the last ten weeks or so. Tom knew Mr Byles a bit by now. Byles was a tough character and a hard-nosed businessman, but he'd always been willing to give someone a chance and had taken on a few young men on probation, especially people like John who'd gained some experience of farming or market gardening while inside.

Byles had made a local reputation as an innovator in market gardening, and Tom had already telephoned him to ask if they could come out and chat to him about John, adding that that they would prefer it if John didn't know. They drove out in Tom's car, trying to look like customers rather than, in Tom's words, policemen disguised as human beings.

Bill Byles saw them in his office, which had probably started life as a potting shed when he set up the business before the war, and was now accompanied by several greenhouses sitting beside carefully tilled vegetable beds. He made his guests a pot of tea and brought it with some mugs into the office on a rusting metal tray.

'Well,' he said, pouring the tea out into the mugs. 'What's young John been up to?'

'Nothing we can prove, Bill. We just wanted to know how he's getting on with you,' said Tom.

Bill took a slurp of his tea and put the mug down carefully on the desk blotter. 'If you'd asked me the same question two weeks ago, I'd have said fine. He's a sandwich short of a picnic and doesn't volunteer much, but he'll do what he's asked. He doesn't mix with the others and doesn't like being told off – but you probably know all that. The others call him the Flowerpot Man because of the way he talks. But in the last fortnight he's gone downhill: bit surly, which is unlike him, and there's an odd hoarding going on. The others are finding little collections of things like flowers or vegetables hidden away in stupid places where he thinks no one will find them. You'd expect him to take the stuff away if he was going to pinch it, but he leaves it there hidden, or forgets about it. When I tackle him about it, he goes into a sulk. Strange lad, really.'

'Perhaps they're short at home?' suggested DC Smith.

'If they were there's no need to act like that. The fact is they're allowed to take some veg or anything we don't need before it goes bad. Says he'll ask his mum. But he never does. Why are you boys out here?'

'Are you going to keep him?' asked Tom, avoiding the question.

'No, I've got to lay him off at the end of the week. A lot of it's seasonal work here and frankly I've had enough of him anyway. Hope this doesn't cause you any problems. Look, you can see him from here.'

Along the side of the vegetable beds ran a field of what looked like young fruit trees, in the middle of which a blonde head moved among the trees, first to the right, then to the left, moving slowly down the row as he did so. But sometimes the head would stop and disappear altogether, like a boat in the waves, and then surface again.

'He's watering,' said Byles. 'He's fine for a time, and then he gets bored and stops. If I go up and see how he's getting on, he thinks I'm spying on him and gets shirty.'

They watched this performance for a minute or two. 'Have you told him he's going yet?' asked Tom.

'Not yet. He'll sulk like hell. I'll give him a week's money in lieu and all the veg he can eat.'

Byles showed them out to their car and gave Tom a couple of cabbages for Mrs Coles. 'Sure you can't tell me what this is all about?' asked Byles. 'Don't tell me it's that girl who was murdered. I wouldn't want that on him. He's okay really – just a bit lacking.'

The two police officers got back into their car, and as they were turning round in the narrow car park they saw John striding up the path to the office at the other end of the car park. 'That's a shame. I don't want him to see us and accuse us of snooping,' said Tom.

But if he had seen them, John didn't show it, walking as usual with his head down and eyes to the ground. His trousers and shoes were soaking wet and he looked agitated, as if he were coming down to report to his boss about something going wrong with the watering.

As they drove back into Bath, DC Smith asked, 'What did you make of that business of Straffen hiding vegetables and stuff?'

'Doesn't surprise me,' replied Tom. 'When he confessed to housebreaking four years ago we found he'd pinched things from houses and then hidden them like he did at Byles's. There wasn't anything of much value, but the point was he didn't take it home, nor did he make any attempt to sell or pass it on. He got sent back from a farm at Winchester to the Hortham Colony a couple of years ago for pinching a bag of walnuts. Pity Byles isn't keeping him on, mind you.'

'I still can't help feeling there's a connection between this and that murder of Christine Butcher in Windsor. It's too much like coincidence. Not that I'm suggesting it was the same man, of course,' said DC Smith.

On 10 July at Windsor, only five days before Brenda's murder, a little girl called Christine Butcher was found strangled with the belt of her own raincoat. The papers had been full of it for weeks afterwards, not only with details of the crime, but of the unsuccessful attempts by the police to find the murderer despite bringing in outside forces to help. The newspapers in the Straffen household would have had every detail of the Windsor murder plastered across the front pages before Brenda's murder in Bath.

'Not the same one, that's for sure,' said Tom. 'No attempt to hide Brenda's body and no sexual attack. They still haven't found anyone for the Windsor one yet, either.'

'It wasn't just strangling, was it? With Brenda he hit her head on the stone as well. Why did he do that?'

'You'll have to ask him, Smithie, when we catch him. We say him – could be a woman, of course. Whoever it is, they're making monkeys out of us, that's for sure.'

Coles and Smith discovered something else significant about the date of the Windsor murder. That was the day on which John Straffen, after reaching the age of 21, had been reassessed by a doctor under the Mental

Deficiency Act. He had assessed John to have a mental age of 10, and suggested he remain on licence for another six months without having to return to Hortham Colony, depending on favourable reports on his work and honesty. John bitterly resented this.

So it was a pity Mr Byles didn't keep John Straffen on at the market garden. Just before he left the office on the following evening, Tom got a phone call from Byles. 'Just thought I'd tell you I gave Straffen his marching orders tonight. He took it badly and blames it all on you.'

'Why us, for God's sake?'

'He saw you at the office and thinks you've told me he's some sort of criminal. I said I'd had plenty of those in my time but they've still got to come to work on time and do the job properly. Anyway, he went off in a huff.'

'Well, maybe it's better he blames us rather than you. I've seen him get bored with jobs before,' said Tom.

Then on the evening of 8 August, at about 8 p.m. in the evening, Mrs Violet Cowley, who happened to be the wife of a Bath police officer, was walking her dog along Bloomfield Road in the south of the city when she noticed a man and a young girl in a field known as the Tumps. They caught her attention for two reasons. First was all the publicity given to the murder of Brenda Goddard in the previous weeks, and second it was unusual to see anyone in this field other than the occasional courting couple – certainly not a man and a young girl so late in the evening.

The man, dressed in a navy-blue suit, and the girl, in a grey cardigan and white-and-blue dress, walked together to the end of the footpath in the field, turned right and went up the slope into the field behind a hedge. Although they were walking side by side, Mrs Cowley recalled, they weren't holding hands.

When she got home she told her detective constable husband what she'd seen, but it all seemed a bit thin for any dramatic action and it was getting too late to do much about it until morning.

But next morning at 7 a.m. they were awoken by an emergency call for DC Cowley to come to the central police station and join a search for a child gone missing the previous evening. When he arrived at the station Cowley reported his wife's story. There was a horrified silence as his seniors realised the description of the girl in the grey cardigan matched the missing girl, and worse still the description of the man in the suit with near blonde hair matched that of the suspect in the last Bath murder, John Thomas Straffen.

They bundled Mrs Cowley, her stomach churning at the prospect of what they might find, into a police car and under her directions drove at full speed up to Bloomfield Road and the field where she had seen the couple.

7

The previous day had been John Straffen's first day of unemployment after leaving the market garden. Mr Byles did offer him a week's wages in lieu of notice, but John decided to work out his notice to give him time to think what to tell everyone at home about why he'd got the sack. He immediately blamed his dismissal on the visit from the police – 'it's a frame-up' he kept repeating – but Mr Byles told him it was nothing to do with the police and he'd give him a reference. But John didn't believe it – why else should the police turn up and he get the sack the next day?

John woke up in the morning and thought it must be Sunday. He even put on his navy-blue suit and decided to go to the cinema, the Forum as usual. It was *Tarzan and the Jungle Queen* and he liked Tarzan films.

The show started at 2 p.m. but he was so late he had to run from Fountain Buildings to the Forum, and it took him ten minutes. He ran down Broad Street, along the High Street past the abbey and into Southgate Street. He met a neighbour on the way, which made him even later. But he only missed the adverts and arrived in time for the Pathé News.

The girl in the pay kiosk recognised him and asked why he was there when it wasn't a Sunday. He didn't have time to answer, shoved his two shillings and a penny through the grill – the 1/6 seats were full – and went straight in. It was very dark and because it was a Tarzan film there were a lot of children in the front rows.

In fact it was children's day and parents were being persuaded by their children to take them to the Tarzan film or let them go by themselves. Another girl was arriving at the cinema on her own and when she found a seat John sat down beside her. When he brought out his sweets he offered her one and she took it.

He asked her name.

'Cicely,' she said.

'Sissy,' John repeated.

'No, C-i-c-e-l-y,' she said and giggled. She felt rather important sitting next to such a big man. This is what the others must mean by a boyfriend.

When the Tarzan film ended they agreed they liked Tarzan films. She told John she was getting on for 10, and from that he worked out she must be 9 years old. 'Do you want to see some more pictures, Sissy?' he asked, offering another sweet.

She nodded. 'There's another good film on at the Scala. I could take you if you like?' he said.

The Scala was in an area of Bath that John knew after working there about three years ago. He knew which bus to get, and didn't seem to mind that the bus conductor was a former workmate and would recognise him. He paid 2d for his fare and 1d for the girl. In fact everyone on the bus would have known about the Brenda Goddard murder and have been on the lookout. But suspicions were allayed by the way they were getting on so well, laughing and talking about the film they'd seen.

Cicely explained to John that the only reason that her mother had let her come out to the cinema on her own was because it was children's day, although she didn't know what children's day meant exactly. She asked him, and he said it probably meant that children could do what they liked for a day. She was wearing a pale blue hair ribbon, a white-and-blue pin-stripe dress with a red belt, and a grey cardigan with glass buttons. Her mother had wanted her to look smart for the cinema before she put her on the bus.

At the Scala John bought two one-shilling tickets for *She Wore a Yellow Ribbon*. John Wayne saved the day with the help of the US cavalry. There was an interval during which John bought them both ice-creams. 'I've got quite a lot of money at the moment because I've just finished work and my boss gave me extra. It's the police that don't let me work,' he mumbled.

She looked up at him, wondering what he was talking about. 'Does your mum tell you to make your bed?' he asked her.

After the show John suggested they go for a walk before they have fish and chips. He knew a good walk, up Englishcombe Lane and through a gate into a field.

It was starting to get dark and Cicely said she wanted to go home. They were lying on the grass near a hedge and John was laughing with her and pinching her nose when they were disturbed by a courting couple out for a walk. The couple passed within a few feet, not realising anyone else was there until they were nearly on them. John stood up and watched the couple walk out through the other end of the field.

When they'd gone he stooped down behind Cicely and put one hand on the back of her neck and the other around the front and squeezed. It wasn't as easy as the first one, and she struggled before she went limp. He didn't feel he had to hit her head or anything and so he left her there where she fell.

John then walked back down into Bath to the old bridge, where he bought fish and chips at the shop by the traffic lights. He was home by 9.45 p.m. Without giving the girl or the films another thought, he had his usual supper of hot milk and bread, made by his mother, went to bed and fell fast asleep as soon as his head hit the pillow.

8

With Mrs Cowley's help it didn't take the police officers long to find Cicely's body. Detective constables Cowley and Smith were sent out to Fountain Buildings to bring in their suspect once they had the full story from Mrs Cowley. They travelled the half mile from Orange Grove to the bottom of Lansdown in a couple of minutes, parking in the Paragon opposite the house and half expecting to see the now familiar figure loping down the raised terrace away from them.

John's mother answered the front door. She looked tired and drawn and not totally surprised at seeing them. 'Excuse us, Mrs Straffen,' said Smithie, 'but we need to see John again.'

'He's in bed,' she replied. 'I'll go up and tell him.'

'We'll have to come with you, I'm afraid.'

The three of them climbed the four flights of stairs together until they reached the top-floor flat, where once inside Mrs Straffen paused for a moment, listening at one of the doors before she knocked.

Although there was no reply they walked in. It was a small room with one window facing onto the street below. In a single bed John Straffen lay asleep, his large feet sticking out at the end of a floral eiderdown. He looked a lot younger than his 21 years, his near blonde locks lying across his pillow and his mouth open. A teddy bear sat up in the bed beside him, its back against the wall and face turned up enquiringly to the police officers, as if demanding what they were doing bursting in at this time of the morning.

Mrs Straffen was having difficulty waking her son. After calling out a couple of times she gently shook him by the shoulder. He opened his eyes looking at the wall, and then, realising there were a number of people in the room, sat up with a start. He was wearing purple striped pyjamas.

'What do you lot want?' he asked, his words slurred with sleep.

'We are police officers, John. We need to take you into the station and ask you to account for your movements yesterday,' said DC Cowley.

'What do you want me for?' John repeated.

There followed a pause while everyone tried to think what to do next. John contemplated making a run for it, while the police officers prepared to jump on him at the first hint of any sudden move.

Mrs Straffen looked around the room for something appropriate to say. 'Would anyone like a cup of tea?' she asked.

'That would be very nice, Mrs Straffen,' said Smithie kindly, and opened the door for her.

Cowley went out with Mrs Straffen and waited outside the door while Smithie remained with John as he dressed. They couldn't afford any last minute dramas such as attempts at escape or even suicide.

Smithie tried to give John as much privacy as possible, and watched him go over to a wardrobe that was impressively hung with a number of jackets, one navy-blue suit, and various pairs of trousers. Smithie remembered the descriptions of the blue suit by the witnesses in both enquiries and decided the suit and any shoes should be brought in with Straffen that morning.

'Better not wear the suit today, John,' said Smithie. 'But I'll bring it with us in case you need it later.'

John opened the window and looked out. 'What sort of day, is it?' he asked. 'I think I'll go for a walk later. I'm not going to the pictures. I'm sick of the pictures.'

Smithie watched all this from the other side of the room, which was sparsely furnished with little sign of the character of the occupant other than a couple of comics thrown onto the chair beside the bed. On the floor was a well thumbed *Beano* annual. Smithie would have bet that had he opened the front page he would find an inscription from John's mother wishing him a happy Christmas or birthday. She looked a kindly woman with worry lines across her face that she probably didn't deserve.

Outside Mrs Straffen had asked DC Cowley if this was more questioning about Brenda Goddard and he nodded that it was. When Smithie brought John into the kitchen, Mrs Straffen poured them all a cup of tea and they sat solemnly around the kitchen table.

'Whatever it is they think you've done,' said Mrs Straffen to her son, 'you should always respect life. It's wrong to interfere with a life, especially a young life. We saw too much of that in the war,' she added, turning to the two police officers, and they nodded solemnly as if some universal truth had been revealed.

John looked down into his teacup and mumbled something inaudible. 'Shall we go, then?' he asked, as casually as suggesting they go for a walk in the park instead of to the police station.

When the policemen had finished their tea they thanked Mrs Straffen and Smithie produced a pair of handcuffs. 'I hope nobody sees him in those,' said Mrs Straffen.

But there was nobody to see them as they walked down to the car and put John in the back seat with Smithie. Cowley carried the blue suit in a cleaner's bag supplied by Mrs Straffen, along with John's shirt, underwear and socks from the previous day. In another bag were three pairs of shoes. John said nothing during the trip and was taken up to Tom Coles's office when they reached Orange Grove.

Tom explained to John why they were taking away his clothes. 'We need to ask you about what you did yesterday, John,' said Tom.

There was a silence. Smithie sat at his desk with his counsel's notebook, waiting for something to write.

'I went to the Forum first, and then to the Scala,' said John at last, without looking up.

'You went to the Forum last time we spoke, didn't you?'

'It was Tarzan this time. It was better. We play Tarzan in The Private. I'm always Tarzan,' said John.

'This is The Private behind Camden Crescent?'

'Yes, I've played there with the children.'

'Let's just stick to yesterday for the moment, John,' said Tom. 'You saw Tarzan at the Forum. Did you meet anyone there?'

John thought about this for a moment, his mouth working before he started speaking. 'I went to the Forum after dinner and sat in the 2/1 seats next to a little girl. After the pictures we came out together and I said to her would she like to see some more pictures. She said she would but she did not have any more money. We caught a bus by the Forum and went to Oldfield Park; I paid the fares. We got off at Moorland Road and went to the Scala. We came out together and walked up the road to a field and along by a hedge. The little girl said she was tired and lay down. I came out and left her.'

After this his chin came back down on his chest and he stared at the desk in front of him, not saying a word.

'What did you do then, John,' asked Tom.

Without looking up he muttered, 'Got fish and chips and went home.'

It was clear he wasn't going to say anything more for the moment and Tom gave the signal for Smithie to go out and make the tea.

Tom didn't try to rush it. He knew John too well for this. He let him cogitate there until Smithie returned with the tea and then tried again. 'When you left the little girl under the hedge, you said she was tired.'

John put down his tea. 'In the field there was a bit of a struggle. She went limp. I was holding her in front by the neck.'

His huge hands worked around the rim of the tea cup as he spoke.

'Did you know the girl?'

'Only from the cinema. She was a bright little girl. Her name was Sissy.'

Tom let him finish his tea. 'What about the other girl, Brenda, the one we spoke about last time at the Crescent.'

'I did her the same,' said John, almost talking to himself this time.

'Do you want to make a written statement about this?' asked Tom.

'You have got no witness. She was picking flowers, and I told her there were plenty higher up. I lifted her over the wall. She never screamed, not even when I squeezed her neck, so I bashed her head against the wall. Here, I'll show you,' said John, leaning forward to put his hands on the desk.

Both officers flinched. 'Would you like your solicitor, or anyone else, to be present when you do this?' asked Tom.

John shook his head and Tom cautioned him. He suggested he demonstrate on PC Smith, who was even more uncomfortable until Tom gave him a look suggesting this was an order rather a request. John turned Smithie in his chair and put his left hand on the back of Smithie's neck, and brought his right hand round to the front of his throat. As he did so, John explained, 'The first one had her back to me when I squeezed her neck, and she went limp quickly, and as she was falling I bashed her head against the wall. I did not feel sorry and forgot about it. I went back over the wall; no one saw me.'

As he finished speaking, John appeared to have forgotten that he had his hands still around Smithie's throat.

John took his hands away and sat back in his seat. His shoulders started to shake and the two officers at first thought he was sobbing – until they realised he was laughing.

'John, do you realise the serious position you are in? We are police officers and you have admitted to strangling two innocent little girls,' Tom reminded him.

'Don't you see,' said John, having trouble containing himself. 'Don't you see, the girls are dead but you cannot prove I did it?'

'We have witnesses. We have Mrs Pullen who saw you in the road outside Camden Crescent; and we have DC Cowley's wife who saw you with Cicely Batstone in the field before you killed her.'

John helped himself to a biscuit from the plate on Smithie's tray. 'They might have seen me in the road and they might have seen me in the field, but no one saw me kill them. You cannot prove it.'

Straffen ate his biscuit with the relish of a man producing the trump card, and smiled in turn at both of his captors, as if to say they might be clever but not clever enough for him.

9

Despite John Straffen's optimism, Tom Coles knew they now had enough in confessions and circumstantial evidence to charge and bring him before the magistrates next morning. The charge that he murdered Cicely Batstone on 8 August 1951 was formally read out to John, to which he made no reply. He was put in a police cell and given something to eat. When word came that he'd like to see Tom Coles again, Tom thought he was going to get a further confession.

Tom went to the cell and lifted the spy hole. John was stretched out on a thin rubber mattress on a bunk staring up at the ceiling. Tom guessed he'd been in this position from the moment he went into the cell two hours ago.

Seeing a prisoner in a police cell is never an easy task. For a start there is nowhere to sit except on the bunk itself, and if this is already occupied by the prisoner, then it creates an atmosphere of intimacy not always welcomed by either party. Tom usually avoided taking any sort of notebook on these occasions as it was a quick way of putting off anyone detained saying anything interesting. For the same reason he preferred not to put them in an interview room where they felt equally constrained. This hadn't prevented Tom having fists and cups of tea and worse thrown at him in the past.

'Got everything you want, John?' Tom asked, perching on the end of the bunk when John wouldn't move his feet.

'That's it, Mr Coles,' said John. 'I wanted to ask if you could bring in a couple of things from home. Could you bring Rupert and my *Beano* book? They're in my room.'

'Rupert?'

'My bear. He's on my bed. He'd like to be here, I think. And could I have my suit back if they've finished cleaning it – I'd like to wear it in court tomorrow?'

'I can get you the book and the bear, but not the suit,' replied Tom tartly. He imagined Smithie's reaction when he was asked to go up to Fountain Buildings and bring in a teddy bear.

'Who will I get in court tomorrow?'

The cell smelt of a mixture of urine and disinfectant. 'It's just a quick hearing tomorrow, only five minutes. They'll probably bring out the mayor and the top brass for you.'

This wasn't just an idle promise to flatter – in notorious cases like this the local mayor or aldermen were invited into court to sit with the magistrates and have a first-hand peek at the monster in the dock.

'The mayor,' John repeated. 'The mayor's coming out to see me? Mum will be pleased.'

'You'll be charged with the second offence, not the first for the moment.'

'But I confessed.'

'I know, but that's the way they do it – one at a time.'

What Tom didn't tell him is that with capital offences attracting the death penalty the prosecution brought one offence at a time on the assumption that, if successful, one charge would be enough.

Tom went back upstairs and found his colleague drinking a cup of tea. 'Smithie – got a little job for you,' he said.

'Yes, sir.'

'Straffen.'

'Yes, sir.'

'He wants his teddy bear.'

'Sir?'

'Get up to the house and get it for him, would you. Get him a change of clothes as well.'

'Is that for the bear or Straffen, sir?'

Tom allowed himself a smile for the first time in days. 'Make sure Mrs Straffen is all right with all this going on. Tell her a bit but not too much yet.'

'Yes, sir.'

'Oh, and he wants his *Beano* annual as well.'

Smithie, who was no longer in uniform, decided to walk up to the house. It had been a long day, a day that had started with finding a body and was now ending picking up a teddy bear, and he wanted some fresh air.

Mrs Straffen answered the door as usual. She looked resigned to whatever he was going to say. She showed him into their living room.

'I've come to collect a few things for John, if that's all right,' said Smithie.

'Will they keep him in tonight?' Mrs Straffen asked.

'A few nights, I'm afraid. They'll charge him with this latest murder of the little girl.'

Mrs Straffen's hand went to her mouth. 'I still can't believe he's had anything to do with those terrible things. It doesn't make sense.'

'He's admitted it now, I'm afraid.'

'He promised he was nothing to do with the first one. I believe him. He's always been such a timid boy, you see. I've always been quite proud of him. John has always gone out there and got jobs. He's so determined, but he doesn't like being told what to do or being told off. He can't really take it from me, but if it's someone at work or the police, someone like that, then he goes in a sulk. We've had him take revenge on officers looking after him in these places where they've sent him over the years.'

Smithie moved uncomfortably in his seat. 'He killed some chickens four years ago, you remember.'

'They were birds, that's not the same.'

'He strangled them. Maybe he was practising.'

Mrs Straffen took a minute to digest all this. 'Well, they didn't charge him.'

'They didn't because he admitted to a number of cases of housebreaking.'

Mrs Straffen sat back in her chair. 'Oh, he's always done that. Steals little things and then hides them. It was the same when he was working down on the farm in Winchester. He stole a bag of walnuts and they sent him back to the Bristol colony. The police have got it in for him. I'm not saying you have here in Bath, but it looks like it, doesn't it? John's convinced all the police want to frame him. "It's a frame-up," he says. He says that every time and I'm beginning to believe him. But not this, not little girls. This is different,' she said, the tears beginning to roll down her cheeks.

'I'm sorry, Mrs Straffen,' said Smithie.

'Oh, it's not your fault, dear. This all really started when we came back from India. John was only 8, but he was so happy out there. We all were, really. That's when the trouble started. His father has had trouble getting work, the children had to change schools, and that was difficult for John because all his little school friends had got used to him out there.

They'd grown up with him. But here in the new school, well, they didn't know what to make of him with his shyness and way of talking. They treated him like some sort of freak and bullied him. It was terrible, really. He's never had a friend back here and he doesn't talk to anyone except us.'

She took him into John's room where she insisted on sorting out a change of clothes for her son while he was away. The room looked even more spartan now, not a picture on the walls, a utility table with one leaf broken where someone had sat on it, and a few comics thrown onto a shelf. The drawers of socks and underwear were surprisingly tidy, but Smithie guessed this was down to Mrs Straffen.

Finally he picked up the annual from the floor and turned to the still unmade bed. 'Is this Rupert?' he asked, pointing to the bear.

'Has he asked for him?'

'His bear and his *Beano*.'

'John's been in a sulk for a couple of days. That's why he needs his bear. It's you lot going out to see his boss at the garden. He reckons you got him the sack.'

Smithie tucked the bear under his arm. 'Yes, well, I'm sorry about that. But we had to see Mr Byles as part of the investigation. But we didn't tell Mr Byles why – I'm afraid John was going to get the sack anyway.'

'You tell him that,' said Mrs Straffen. 'It wouldn't surprise me if John is causing all this trouble to get back at us. He didn't like me telling him to make his bed the other day.'

She found a bag and placed the bear and book inside. Mrs Straffen added an apple and a liquorice sherbet she'd found hidden in John's underwear drawer. She saw Smithie down to the front door.

'Thanks for coming up for his things. Whatever terrible things he's done, he's only a child really. I've always had to tell myself that,' she said, and closed the door quietly behind him.

10

Next morning the queue to get into the public gallery at Bath Magistrates' Court for the first hearing stretched out of the Guildhall and into the High Street. The police managed to squeeze eighty members of the public into the court, packing them as tightly as sardines. A quarter of the spectators were women. The courtroom was large enough to seat this sort of number, constructed in the traditional style of police courts with a high ceiling and raised dais at the front from which the magistrates could gaze down to the solicitors or barristers representing the accused, the officer representing the police, and behind them at eye level the defendant in the dock. Prisoners on remand would be brought up from the police cells into the dock, while defendants on bail sat in a row on a bench next to the dock waiting to be called.

British justice will never be hurried and Friday mornings at Bath Magistrates' Court were no exception. The business of the day started with licensing applications, usually bar extensions for a party or wedding. So when a local publican stood up at 10 a.m. sharp to make his application, he was confronted by the mayor of Bath, an alderman and his wife, and two other magistrates, not to mention representatives of most of the local and national press packed into seats near the door. On one side of him sat a barrister and two solicitors, and on the other side the chief constable of Bath. Only the dock in this sea of upturned faces remained empty.

The publican was granted his extension as speedily as possible after no objections were offered from the chief constable, and a buzz of expectancy went around the court. When John Straffen appeared in the dock between two police officers and handcuffed to one of them, it was almost as if he hadn't noticed he was in court at all. His sports jacket was crumpled and his face unshaven. He was in the middle of explaining something to his escorts, and finished what he was saying without looking up at the bench. His hair was combed straight back over his head and wetted so that it had lost its colour, and his face was puffy through lack of sleep.

Only when the clerk to the court asked him if his name was John Thomas Straffen did he raise his eyes shyly to the bench and try to work out why so many people were sitting up there with glittering chains around their necks. Only then did he remember what Mr Coles had said about the mayor coming. John was no stranger to this court, but never in the company of so many people – he assumed they'd come to see the mayor.

As the charge was read out to him, that on 8 July 1951 he did unlawfully kill Cicely Batstone at Bath with malice aforethought, John looked back at the public gallery to see if his mother was there but he couldn't see her. Then he glanced at the row of waiting defendants to see if there was anyone he recognised, only then returning to the clerk before being told he could sit down.

During the four-minute hearing the chief constable read out a résumé of the facts of the case and asked for a seven-day adjournment to allow the prosecution to prepare its case, fighting to make himself heard over the din outside in Orange Grove from the crowd gathered for the hearing. John's solicitor rose to say he had no objection to the adjournment, and asked if his client might see his mother at the police station before he was taken over to Bristol Prison where he would remain on remand. This gave the bench something to do, and most of the consultation was made with the alderman's wife, who as a woman presumably knew about mothers wanting to see their sons. She nodded back at the solicitor and then at John with a sympathetic smile. John stared back with his characteristic half grin.

He was remanded formally for seven days without any application for bail. With that the prisoner disappeared with his escort back down the steps.

He was taken back to his cell in the basement of the station, given a cup of tea and told to get ready to meet his mother upstairs. Meanwhile Mrs Straffen had to be found in the crowd outside in Orange Grove.

She had elected to remain outside rather than come into court, as had Mr Pullen, Brenda Goddard's stepfather. It was left to PC Smith to go out and find her in a mob that by now was ready to lynch anyone with the name of Straffen.

He soon found her on the fringe of the crowd, obviously upset, with her niece at her side doing her best to comfort her. Smithie didn't have to say anything, just nodding to answer the question as to whether the court had agreed to her seeing her son. He steered her back through the crowd to a side door in the station, and then upstairs to a small interview room looking out at the side of the Imperial Hotel next door, where there was little chance of anyone seeing them.

The police felt it was more appropriate that mother and son met in the comparative civility of an interview room rather than in a cell, but it was agreed that Smithie would remain handcuffed to John during the meeting, with an officer placed outside the room just in case. John Straffen was a big man and powerfully built and, while the chance of escape was remote from the police station, there was no knowing how he might react to meeting his mother in these circumstances.

Smithie found John as usual stretched out on his bed in the cell, apparently reluctant to see his mother at all. He attached the handcuffs and they moved awkwardly upstairs, where they parked themselves opposite Mrs Straffen at the table, Smithie sitting at the end of the table with his left wrist on the table attached to John's right wrist, their two hands moving in unison every time John pushed his hair back or raised a hand to cough.

Mrs Straffen looked hard at her son, while he remained with his eyes down on the table and his mouth hanging slack. Instinctively she put out a hand to touch his. 'What on earth is going on, John?' she asked.

'I killed those two girls,' said John, without looking up.

'What do you mean?' she asked.

'I killed the two little girls. I've confessed.'

Mrs Straffen thought about this for a moment and gripped his hand. 'Look at me, John. Why did you do that?' she asked. 'I can't believe you'd do a thing like that.'

John in turn thought about this, raised his head to look at his mother for the first time and asked, 'Did they come and collect Rupert and the book?'

This time both Mrs Straffen and Smithie nodded, and when it became obvious John wasn't going to say much else, Mrs Straffen asked where they would take him. She was told Bristol Prison at Horfield, and John was taken back down to the cells, where he was reunited with Rupert and his *Beano* annual.

Whenever anyone looked through the spy hole in the cell in the following hour before transport was arranged to Bristol, they saw John on his bunk reading his *Beano*, his teddy bear sat up against the wall next to him.

The scene at Bristol Prison during the two months of remand changed very little. John proved a model prisoner; he took his exercise and generally kept himself to himself. In fact the prison staff rather took him under their wing as someone generally vulnerable, both to himself as a mental defective, and from other prisoners who took unkindly to child killers. The answer was virtual solitary confinement: that suited everyone.

The person who had the most difficulty was his solicitor. His client was reluctant to give any instructions despite facing the death penalty at a trial fast approaching in October. John expressed no regret for what he'd done – if the murders had inconvenienced the police then they'd served their purpose. There was no sympathy for the families, and no empathy with the victims in what they must have gone through in those last terrifying moments of their short lives.

So it came as some relief to a defence team without a defence when the prosecution announced they considered John Straffen unfit to enter a plea at his forthcoming trial. This defence was usually reserved for insane defendants unable to give instructions to their lawyers, and while in a capital offence like murder they escaped the death penalty, it meant being detained at His Majesty's pleasure in a secure institution like Broadmoor.

The trial was fixed for Wednesday 17 October 1951 at the Taunton Assizes, part of the western circuit where judges would come into the city for periods of a few weeks to try the more serious cases, and then move to the next assize on the circuit, in this way creating as much continuity in sentencing as possible.

This was the first time that John had been tried before a judge and jury. He was brought down on the previous day from Bristol and spent the night in the cells reading comics and sucking peppermints supplied by the police staff.

One of the ironies of John Straffen's criminal career was that for a man of limited intelligence his case seemed to attract some of the best brains in the legal profession as counsel in court, including a serving Solicitor General and future Law Lord. Today it was the turn of the Honourable Ewen Montagu for the prosecution, the son of a peer and the creator of the major wartime deception codenamed 'Operation Mincemeat', when the Germans were fooled into believing the Allies would invade Greece and Sardinia in 1943 rather than Sicily, which was the true objective. This was achieved by planting 'secret' documents on a body off the coast of Spain and allowing it to be washed up on the shore, where it found its way to the Germans.

Ewen Montagu was also junior counsel for the defence in the notorious case of Alma Rattenbury in 1935 when she was charged with murdering her elderly husband in Bournemouth with her young lover George Stoner. Stoner was convicted and sentenced to death, while Rattenbury was acquitted but committed suicide a few days later. The public was so outraged that a large petition saved Stoner from the gallows and he emerged from prison after only seven years.

Now John Straffen popped up in the dock, chatting as usual to his warders as the twelve-man jury was sworn in. He still wore the same grey jacket and coloured shirt he'd been wearing at Bath Magistrates' Court in August. It was then left to Mr Montagu to call his one and only witness, Dr Peter Parkes, the medical superintendant at Bristol Prison.

Mr Montagu asked Dr Parkes if he had supervised John Straffen during his period of custody in Bristol. 'I have visited him on several occasions and am familiar with his medical record,' said Parkes, opening a file in front of him but not needing to consult it. 'He has been certified as a mental defective on several occasions. There was an occasion when he attacked a 13-year-old girl four years ago after an argument and threatened to strangle her, but then he ran off before he did any real harm and so this seems to have been dismissed as childish behaviour rather than anything more sinister. There was another occasion when he strangled some chickens belonging to the father of a girl with whom he'd had another argument.'

'Has his condition improved or got worse while he's been in custody?' asked Mr Montagu.

'Well, I'd think it's been about the same. He's a person of low intelligence, about that of a 10 year old, and has spent most of the time reading children's comics and adventure stories. He certainly doesn't seem very worried about his situation, which considering the seriousness of the charges and the possible penalties you might find surprising.'

'Have you discussed with him why he might have committed these offences?'

'As far as I can see it was to annoy the police, whom he blames for most of the things that have gone wrong in his life, to include his recent loss of a job.'

Montagu picked up his notes. 'And after the offences did Straffen buy fish and chips and eat these happily on the way home?'

'I believe he did,' replied Dr Parkes, and turned towards the public gallery where there was a clicking of tongues.

'And as a result have you come to the conclusion that he is not only certifiable, but is a feeble-minded person and is not fit to plead because he does not know what it means to do so, is unable to instruct counsel, and does not know what they are for, and would not be able to take part in the trial?' asked Montagu.

'That is right, my lord,' replied Parkes, looking over to the judge.

Mr Justice Oliver thanked Dr Parkes and turned immediately to the jury as if there was no time to lose. 'Members of the jury, you have heard the evidence of Dr Parkes this morning concerning the tragic case of the murder of this little girl. In turn I am directing you to find the prisoner John Thomas Straffen unfit to enter a plea to this charge, and this is because he cannot understand the course of these proceedings to make a proper defence, or to understand the evidence, or to give proper instructions to his counsel. One might as well, members of the jury, try a baby in arms.'

This picture of trying a baby in arms resonated with the jury who, looking at a six foot man in the dock with his chin on his chest, his mouth falling open and his eyes staring dully in front of him, wondered how much was going on in that head under the unkempt locks of hair, and that anyone murdering a little girl in somewhere as respectable as Bath was probably out of his mind anyway.

As directed, the jury duly entered a verdict of unfit to plead and the judge dispatched the prisoner to Broadmoor Institution 'until His Majesty's pleasure be known'. As the judge gave his directions, John stood in the dock, smiling affably back at him, and was taken down the steps from the dock to the cells, where he would in normal circumstances have disappeared from public view forever.

But nothing about John Straffen was ever going to be normal, and in less than six months he was back on the front page of every national newspaper, the object of public outrage, facing the death penalty for a second time in his life, and the subject of debate between Prime Minister Winston Churchill and his Cabinet.

11

When they told John in the car that they were getting near Broad-moor, he started taking an interest in the journey. He'd got the idea it was out in the countryside and not, like Horfield, in the middle of a city. They were travelling up a hill, past a lot of houses and then through a wood, when one of the officers said, 'There you are, Straffen, this is going to be your new home.'

On first sight it looked more like a fort in a John Wayne movie: great big walls and a huge gateway that you drove through with guards coming out to open the doors and ask who you were. But when the crashing of gates and loud voices had finished and they were inside, the place didn't look so much like a fort or a prison, but more like one the institutions, such as Besford Court or Hortham Colony, where John had already spent a third of his life, large Victorian buildings with lawns and trees and benches.

The first thing Straffen got was a room of his own, and they called it a room, not a cell. Then over a few weeks of what they called assessment John started to relax a little and talk to the doctors who were asking him questions. That was already different to prison; they seemed more inter-ested in you here. He enjoyed meals in the dining hall and sitting next to the other patients – they called them patients and not prisoners.

John must have answered a lot of questions right because they moved him to another building and he was allowed to walk around in the airing courts and do some work in the vegetable garden. He told them he'd worked in the market garden at Bathampton before the police got him the sack.

They gave him pills that made him feel a bit calmer. But the only way he could show them he wasn't a murderer would be to get out and not murder anyone – that way they couldn't say he was dangerous any more. He knew they wouldn't let him out of the gate, so he'd have to find a way of getting out by himself without them knowing, where he could walk around freely and pay a few calls on local people and perhaps have tea with them, and they'd say there's a normal sort of bloke who shouldn't be shut up in that place with a lot of madmen.

The men's day room at Broadmoor was a cavernous area on the ground floor of the building looking out over neatly trimmed lawns and gravel pathways. It was the size of the lounge in the York Hotel in Bath he could see from his window at home. Some of the patients sat alone or in a group reading or playing cards, while others sat staring vacantly out of the vast windows. The patients wore denim trousers and thick wool jackets, while an attendant standing near the door wore a dark tunic and peaked cap, and a male nurse in a white coat seated under the window kept an eye on things.

John was sat at one table with three other patients playing bridge. While not brilliantly proficient at the game, this gave him the best chance to talk and live a more sociable life than he had had in his 21 years so far. He'd been taught the basic rules of bridge by his friend Dick Whitcombe, who took care not to criticise him if he messed up a bid, like he did once when John stalked off in a sulk and refused to play for the rest of the day. But next morning he was his genial self and seemed to have forgotten and forgiven.

What was different to a casual observer was the pace of life where everything happened at half speed: moves on the chequers board or playing hands of cards took twice as long as they should, books took a year to read in the atmosphere of a public library, and conversations were conducted in hushed undertones in case you said something you shouldn't and a nurse heard. But time was something they weren't short of.

John and Dick Whitcombe were playing against Jock and Tony, who between them had served over twenty years in Broadmoor. Jock was a stockily built Scot who'd twice come near a transfer date to a 'B' security grade psychiatric hospital after years of co-operative behaviour, only to blow it when he got up on the roof and started throwing tiles at people down below. Friends said it was because he liked it too much in Broadmoor and didn't want to be moved. Tony was a deeper one: prematurely bald with a funny eye, it was taken for granted that he'd never leave Broadmoor, although no one knew exactly what he'd done outside and he wasn't going to say.

The topic of conversation during the game had been escape, following the film shown the previous evening in the Central Hall. A big cheer had gone up when the prisoners of war finally made it out of the German camp and struggled to the surface, only to be caught later after running out of food and luck.

John opened the bidding so recklessly his partner paid little attention to the cards he might really hold.

'I suppose we could dig a tunnel,' said John, as if he'd been thinking about it all day.

'You wouldn't get further than that lot last night,' said Dick.

'I'm quite near the wall working in the vegetables. I could tunnel out through the potatoes.'

Before he made a bid, Jock put his cards face down on the table and looked out of the window. 'If you wanted to escape from here there's no need to tunnel – you just jump over the wall,' he said slowly.

'Oh yeah,' said Dick. 'You just jump over the wall. Why doesn't anyone do it, then?'

'They don't do it because they don't want to. Why should they? They'd bring you back like a dog on a lead, shove you into a kennel somewhere and stop your biscuits for a bit.'

'Well, I'd like to escape,' said John. 'I'd like to escape and watch their faces while they search around looking for me all day while I was miles away.'

'If you were miles away then you wouldn't be able to watch them,' said Tony, speaking for the first time that afternoon. 'Where would you go anyway, John – back to Bath? They'd spot you a mile off.'

John thought about this. 'I'd go to Manchester.'

They all looked at him. 'Who do you know in Manchester?'

'No one – that's why I'd go there.'

John hadn't a clue where Manchester was, but he had a point. It was a long way away and no one would recognise him. John wasn't stupid on some things.

'Anyway, I know where you can get over the wall,' said Jock.

They looked at him. 'Where's that, Jock?' asked Dick.

'The surgery,' he replied. 'If you could get through the surgery then there's a shed with a roof only a couple of feet from the top of the wall and then you're over.'

They all put down their cards and thought about this. The surgery was an old disused room but still on the cleaning rota, which included John on Wednesdays.

'But how do you get up onto the roof?' asked John. 'Someone would have to help you.'

The idea of getting out and running for it all the way to Manchester appealed to him. He could make a few friends on the way – now he knew how to make friends – and they would tell him where Manchester was and help him get there. The police would have to spend days looking for him and they would never think of looking in Manchester.

John was on cleaning duties in the surgery area with Dick and Mr Cash, a 68-year-old attendant who let you get on with it if you didn't cause him any bother. John made them all a cup of tea at 11 a.m. and Mr Cash liked talking about what he'd done with his grandchildren over the weekend.

'There are some drums of stuff stashed outside the surgery next to the shed. I reckon a big boy like you, John, could hop onto one of those and get up on the roof without any trouble,' said Jock.

They picked up their cards and went on playing. 'If it's so easy, Jock, then why haven't you done it?' asked Dick gravely.

'Why do I want to get out?' asked Jock. 'There's nothing for me out there.'

'I'd like to get out,' said John. 'If you get out then they can't put you back in here.'

Now it was their turn to look at John. 'Where did you get that from, John?' asked Jock.

'Those are the rules. If you get out then they can't put you back in Broadmoor.'

'They'll bring you back and you'll lose all your privileges. What's the point?'

John made another wild bid and Dick groaned, though not too loudly in case it annoyed John.

'Do you think we should tell the Escape Committee?' asked John.

'You've been watching too many films,' said Dick.

In fact there was an Escape Committee in Broadmoor and had been for some time, but the proposals put forward to the committee were mostly fantasies cooked up in the middle of the night by escapees who wouldn't have known what to do if they ever made it to the outside. The chairman of the committee was an ex-company director who patiently listened to ideas of bomb making and mass poisonings that were so alarming he sometimes had to report them to the staff who in turn carried out searches in case there was a grain of truth to the plots.

Then there was Jock and a friend who instead of tunnelling into the ground had decided to go upwards through the ceiling, and then another ceiling, and then another, onto the roof where they remained for two days hurling slates at anyone trying to remove them. The sleeping quarters below had to be evacuated and forty patients ended up sleeping on mattresses on the ground floor out of range of the missiles. This particularly appealed to John as it wasted the staff's time for a couple of days.

Next Wednesday John took more interest than usual in the surgery. As he filed into the building between Dick and Mr Cash, he took particular care not to look too carefully out of the back window or door in case Mr Cash became suspicious. But when John thought they'd been dusting for long enough he asked if he could go outside to shake out his duster. Once outside he darted round the corner and immediately saw the two drums of disinfectant pushed up against the main wall and a few feet away from the shed. Once on a drum he reckoned someone with his height wouldn't find it difficult to scramble onto the roof, and up the slates to the outside wall. It would be a long drop down the other side but he was willing to risk it.

John had hardly finished considering his master plan when Dick put his head out of the door with a look that asked why he was there at all and not already over the wall and miles away. 'Mr Cash asked what you are doing and to come back inside,' he said. He held the door open for John, and he returned with his duster.

Later in the day room Dick asked him what he'd found.

'Jock's right. It looks easy,' said John.

'Mr Cash will miss you in about half a minute.'

'You could knock him out,' suggested John enthusiastically.

'Like hell I will. I'm not getting involved with this. I give you about half an hour and you'll be back here,' said Dick.

'The only thing that worries me is the drop the other side,' said John.

'That's all right. I'll come round and catch you,' said Dick.

John considered this. 'I thought you said you weren't getting involved?'

12

For the next week John considered his chances of escaping. He knew there were trees outside the walls and they would give him a good bit of cover, and that at the bottom of the hill there were houses and they would give him the chance to show he could act normally without hurting anybody. If there were children playing in the street or garden, then all the better because he could talk to them and walk away without harming them. If they ever found out that was John Straffen who escaped from Broadmoor, then they would say they felt completely safe with him as they talked and played.

But if he was going to act normal then he would have to look normal. He would not look normal in a Broadmoor uniform, but there he hit on a good idea. If he wore his suit underneath his uniform, then once he was out he could get rid of the uniform, in the woods perhaps, and then appear the other side of the woods in his suit like any other young local man asking for a cup of water on a summer's day.

His suit was hanging on the rack at the back of his cupboard in his room. They were only allowed to wear their suits on special occasions, like show performances by the Broadhumoorists, the hospital drama group, or the Christmas carol service.

John decided against digging a tunnel because you would be so muddy by the time you got out there would be no way you would look normal.

So the following Wednesday, when he was next due to be on the surgery cleaning rota, he got up early and brought out the suit from the back of the wardrobe. John kept on his pyjamas because he thought he might be cold if he had to stay out overnight. He came down to breakfast wearing three layers of clothing – his pyjamas, suit and his work clothes – and he was prepared to tell anyone asking why he was dressed like the Michelin Man that he had a bad cold and didn't fancy getting it any worse outside.

John ate twice as much as usual at breakfast and twice as much at lunch to keep him stored up for the journey ahead. At lunch he leaned over to Jock and whispered, 'If you don't see me at supper it's because I've gone over the top.'

'So you're going to have a bash at it, are you?' said Jock.

'You don't mind, do you?'

'What's the plan?'

'I'm on cleaning rota with Mr Cash. I go out of doors and shake my duster and that's my chance of getting over the wall.'

'Then what do you do?'

'Then I run for it,' said John, tackling a second helping of potatoes.

'I thought you said you were going to Manchester,' interrupted Dick.

'That's right. I'm going to make friends and they'll take me to Manchester.'

'Do you know how far Manchester is, John?'

'They'll know where it is.'

'Don't bet on it,' said Dick. He was doubtful about the whole plan. He saw John jumping over the wall and breaking an ankle at the bottom, then leaving it to him to explain to Mr Cash how much he really knew about the plan. Dick was practising in his own mind how to tell Mr Cash that John was missing after going out to shake his duster. Dick felt sorry for Cash and didn't want to get him into trouble: he was a kind old buffer, past retirement age and genuinely concerned for his patients and their welfare. He'd probably get disciplined, or even dismissed, for letting John out of his sight and that wouldn't be much to tell his grandchildren at the weekend.

John was worried about the escape film they'd seen. 'They won't shoot me, will they?' he asked.

'With luck they will,' said Dick.

'Come with me, Dick,' said John. 'All you do is let me go out first with the duster. I'll ask Mr Cash if I can, then when I don't come back soon you tell Cash you are going to ask me when I'm coming back in. You follow me over and we're out. Think of the fun we could have.'

'Sorry, John, you're on your own. The only reason I'd come with you is to look after you. You're going to do something stupid, I can feel it.'

John looked at his friends with that half grin and slack mouth they'd all got so used to over the six months they'd been with him. 'Who wants my *Beano* annual?' he asked.

'Are you taking Rupert with you?' asked Jock.

John closed his mouth in concentration in trying to answer a question he'd put to himself so many times. 'Rupert likes it here. He's going to stay and look after things. I'll send for him later.'

'Why don't you tuck yourself up with your bear and your annual and forget about escaping?' said Dick.

'I want to meet my friends again. The police don't like that.'

'Which friends were those, John?' asked Jock.

'My friends in The Private. No one knew about it, not even their parents. You didn't even have to make your bed. The police didn't know about it and so couldn't come snooping and all that sort of thing.'

'But they did come snooping, didn't they, John?' said Jock.

'They should have stayed out of it, then they wouldn't have found things they didn't like.'

They'd all heard this a hundred times, but one particular phrase John had found in his *Beano* annual had become a mantra for them. 'You led them a song and dance, eh John?' they chimed.

'That's right, I sang and they danced,' replied John, and banged his fist on the table to make the cutlery rattle.

Tony, who'd kept quiet during all this, took John by the arm. 'Just don't do it again, John. Some people in here have got kiddies of their own and they'll twist your bloody head off if you get up to your tricks again,' he said.

'That's right, Tony,' replied John, the smile disappearing.

'You do that again and they'll have you dancing on the end of a rope.'

'Okay, Tony.'

'And if they don't do it, I'll do it for them,' said Tony, taking his hand away and getting up to leave the table.

John let Tony get out of earshot. 'I only got caught because I told the police. They couldn't prove a thing otherwise.'

'Not the version I read,' said Jock, who'd read the court reports in the paper before John's arrival.

'But none of them saw me do anything.'

'A witness doesn't have to see you commit a crime, you daft brush.'

'That's why they sent me here, you see.'

'They sent you here because they certified you like the rest of us. Otherwise they'd have strung you up, like Tony said.'

'I was too clever for them.'

Dick looked at the clock on the dining room wall. 'Well, you can show us how clever you really are in about fifteen minutes. We're on cleaning rota with Mr Cash in the surgery, so get your bag packed and your shoes polished for the great escape.'

John went back up to his room to make last-minute preparations for the escape, but all he could think of doing was combing his hair so that he would look neat when it came to hitching a lift to Manchester. He made Rupert comfortable on his bed and told him he would send for him when he got to Liverpool, and then realised he meant Manchester.

Next he visited the toilet as there might not be a toilet handy once he got over the wall. Once he'd done that he went over to the basins and had a good long drink of water as getting a drink was likely to be difficult on the run, until he realised that would only make him need a toilet all the more.

Then he went down to the stores and drew a bucket and mop for cleaning duties, together with a large duster made up of a shredded blanket. Dick was waiting for him outside the surgery with his bucket and mop, and presently Mr Cash arrived.

Mr Cash was someone they all liked. His uniform jacket didn't quite fit around his stomach and so he preferred to wear it with the buttons undone, along with a peaked cap that made him look slightly younger by hiding his balding head, and a pair of boots with spit and polished toecaps as a leftover from his training in the army. He'd decided to retire in two years and counted the days with more enthusiasm than the patients.

He took one look at John and laughed out loud. 'What's the matter with you, Straffen?' he asked.

'I've got a bit of a cold, Mr Cash. Thought I'd put on a few extras and sweat it out.'

Cash looked at him again. 'You've combed your hair. You must be ill.'

'Always like to look tidy, Mr Cash.'

Mr Cash produced a bunch of keys and opened the door into a large room that probably hadn't been entered since the last time it was cleaned a week ago. There was a sink in the far corner and John and Dick went over to fill their buckets and throw in some detergent from a container on the shelf over the basin. They set to work on the floor while Mr Cash held forth on his favourite subjects: what he was planning to do in retirement and what his grandchildren were up to at the weekend.

Once the floor was washed it was the turn of the dusters. John was worried that he wasn't going to find enough dust to merit having to ask to go outside and shake the duster. But the windowsill was filthy, mainly because on normal cleans he'd avoid it because it was so dirty.

As he ran the duster over the windowsill he glanced out of the window to check the weather, but all he could see was the wall blotting out the sky. He now couldn't wait to get over the wall to the outside where he could meet his friends and run and do all the things he'd wanted to do over the last six months. They could do what they liked with him if they caught him, take away his privileges and make him start again in the admissions block. They could hang him if they wanted; it couldn't be any worse than being cooped up in here being told what to do all day.

'Excuse me, Mr Cash,' he said.

'Yes, lad, what is it?' asked Cash.

'Can I go out and shake my duster?' He held it out to Mr Cash to show him how filthy it was. He'd done this last week just to get Cash used to the idea. To do this he had to use the back door to the room, pulling back two bolts and an internal dead lock.

Mr Cash looked at the duster, nodded and went on talking about the cruise he and his good wife had booked for the day he retired, although they couldn't take the grandchildren because that would be in the middle of their school term.

John hoped that Cash would remember he used the back door as he crossed the room holding the duster out in front of him at arm's length. He whistled a tuneless tune in the way he'd rehearsed a hundred times in his room.

John pulled back the bolts and then struggled with the large key in the rusty lock. 'Straffen,' Cash called out.

'Yes, Mr Cash,' said John without turning round.

'That door.'

'Yes, Mr Cash?'

'Make sure you don't lock yourself out,' said Mr Cash and roared with laughter at his own joke.

John turned the handle and was out.

The first thing he did was to go round the corner to the outside wall and half roll, half push one of the disinfectant drums up to the side of the shed to give himself the best chance of getting onto the roof.

He'd just finished this and clambered onto the roof when Dick emerged from the back door. 'Mr Cash wants to know when you're coming back in,' shouted Dick, loud enough to let Mr Cash know that everything was under control.

'Tell him I'm shaking my duster. Back in a jiff,' John shouted back at the same volume so that Mr Cash could hear.

The roof slates were slippery and at first he neither went up nor down as his feet pedalled away trying to get a grip. Then by bringing his knees nearly up to his chin he found a better grip by placing the soles of his boots flat on the slates, and he slowly made his way up the roof to the top of the wall. With both hands now on the wall he carefully poked his head over the top. He could hear the birds singing and the sound of the wind in the trees, before he had to bring his head smartly back for a car passing in the road below.

As luck would have it, the height at this part of the outer wall was 10 rather than 20 feet, but even 10 feet looks a long way down when you have to jump. John clambered over the top and, partly to avoid having to look down and partly to reduce the drop as much as possible, he hung on to the top of the wall and let his legs dangle until his arms were at full stretch. He hung there for a second or two until his arms ached so much he closed his eyes and let go.

13

John Straffen entered the free world feet first with a splintering crash. He'd fallen through the fire hydrant cover at the bottom of the wall, where his solid work boots probably saved him a broken ankle. Like a gymnast misjudging an exercise on the horse, he rolled onto the grass in a heap and stood up to attention as soon as possible in an attempt to look normal.

John glanced at the main gates, and then back up at the top of the wall, and when no one called out or blew a whistle, he straightened his clothes and stepped down to the road heading for the cover of the trees on the other side. He'd decided not to run as that would look even more suspicious – he learnt that years ago when he'd escaped from youth institutions. He knew no alarm or siren would go off here because there wasn't one at Broadmoor, so no one outside would be aware of an escape. This would give him a good start if he acted normally.

The first step towards normality was getting rid of the work clothes, and so once he was in the trees, John stopped to shed his jacket and denim trousers and, like a butterfly emerging from a chrysalis, stepped forward smartly dressed in his suit and white shirt. Only the work boots spoiled the effect but he'd given them a good polish in the morning. He bundled the old clothes together and hid them under a bush, gave his hair a quick comb, dusted his boots again and felt ready to face the world.

He was already sweating profusely in the heat of the spring afternoon and was glad to be in the deep shade of the trees. Instinctively he starting walking downhill, and when he came to where the trees cleared for a row of hospital staff houses, he paused before turning to move behind the houses, sticking to the cover of the woods for as long as he could.

But before he did he noticed two attendants, unmistakable in their uniforms, on bicycles pedalling down the hill looking around and calling out to each other when they thought they saw something.

There was no time to lose, and John calculated that as long as he was out of sight in the trees then he might as well run for it.

Suddenly he was John Wayne escaping from the fort at the top of the hill. He'd shed his uniform but he still wore his cavalry boots. They'd already sent out a couple of men on horses to bring him back, but he'd outsmart and outrun them. He'd be welcomed by every lady of the house as a stranger in town and given a glass of water or even a cup of tea. He ran through beds of bluebells under the trees, sending squirrels running up the trees and scolding birds into the sky. If there were Indians behind the trees, they left him alone, recognising another fugitive.

Then he heard the sound of traffic up ahead. He stopped running and walked cautiously on another twenty yards and found he'd come to the edge of the wood. Ahead of him was the distinct outline of a road, and on the other side were houses.

This was where he could put it all to the test. He pulled down his jacket and did up the buttons. Then he gave his hair another comb. He tried to think how normal people looked and how they might come out of a wood and walk up someone's drive and ask for a glass of water.

Suddenly he had a picture of all his little friends in The Private in Bath, like a school photo, only they were waving to him and calling out his name. What stories he could tell them now he was free and explain why he wasn't around for the last few months to play with them and have adventures.

He didn't want them to think he'd deserted them or anything rude like that.

Over the road Mrs Doris Spencer was pottering in her back garden near her greenhouse at her detached house in Pinewood Avenue, Crowthorne. She was taking the opportunity of the fine weather to plant out sweetpeas and chrysanthemums.

When she heard the click of the front gate she stopped her work and stood to look down the drive to make sure the gate was shut again. Sometimes delivery boys would forget to close it despite a notice on the gate and run the risk of letting one of her dogs out. She was expecting a delivery of dog food that afternoon and usually they remembered the gate.

But it wasn't the delivery boy – in fact it wasn't a boy at all but a tall, gangling young man in his early twenties, dressed in a blue suit and with large feet, sweating profusely despite his casual amble up the drive.

'Good afternoon,' said Mrs Spencer pleasantly. 'Can I help you?'

'I am a stranger,' replied John Straffen, mumbling rather but quite coherent.

'Yes, I can see that,' said Mrs Spencer airily. 'But I am afraid this is private property, and there is no through road except for a small path leading to the village.'

'I see,' said John. 'Well, could I have a drink of water?'

Mrs Spencer hesitated for a moment. Not because she was uncharitable, but because there were still young men drifting around the country in their demob suits unable to find work and she simply couldn't find it in her heart to turn them away. It was rarer here on the outskirts of Crowthorne, but this one was wearing a cheap suit and had an inane grin that worried her. Still, he looked harmless enough.

When she went into the kitchen to get him a drink of water, she hadn't expected him to follow her, but he loped after her like one of her dogs, his tongue almost hanging out as if they were returning from a walk in the woods. But once inside she felt more secure: two of the dogs were in the sitting-room and two in the kitchen, looking up with ears pricked when she appeared with a stranger rather than the pet food man.

John sat down at the kitchen table and looked back at the two Alsatian dogs, which remained lying down but were now on alert. He studied them with interest but without any sign of fear. 'Would they attack anyone?' he asked.

'Yes, if they were provoked,' Mrs Spencer replied carefully. 'Would you like a cup of tea?'

John nodded without a word of thanks. 'How far is it to Reading?' he asked.

'About ten miles.'

'Oh,' said John.

'There's bus stop in the village,' said Mrs Spencer. 'You can get a bus to Reading.'

John shrugged his shoulders and Mrs Spencer guessed he hadn't any money. As she said it, John realised the fact too. Trouble was they didn't use cash in Broadmoor and even at Bath he only got a bit of pocket money from his mother to go to the pictures and get chips. He looked down at the kitchen table and Mrs Spencer felt rather sorry for him. There was no guessing what these young men had done in the war and the sort of terrible things they'd seen.

She was just about to offer him some money to get to Reading, when he starting asking about the various roads out of the village and where they led.

'Oh, Wokingham and Camberley,' she replied.

'And the village,' he added. 'Has it got a cinema?'

'I'm afraid not. We're a little bit too small for our own cinema, but Reading has. Do you enjoy the pictures?' she asked.

'I like the pictures,' John said slowly, slurring his speech now he was having to remember words he'd planned to use on the outside. 'Most of my friends like the pictures. I go every week. Sundays, usually.'

'What films do you like best?' Mrs Spencer asked, pouring the tea.

'Oh, Tarzan. Anything really.'

John took a sip of his tea, having trouble with Mrs Spencer's cups due to his large fingers. 'Is Broadmoor Institution far from here?' he asked, like a tourist asking what other attractions he might visit while he was here.

'About half a mile,' she replied.

'Is that all?' he said, disappointed that was all the distance he'd put behind him. He'd been running hard for what felt like a long time, but that didn't mean he'd been running in a straight line. 'Patients escape sometimes, do they?'

'Yes, sometimes,' said Mrs Spencer, starting to feel uncomfortable about her guest, not least because her husband worked at Broadmoor. It'd been on the tip of her tongue to say so when he first mentioned Broadmoor but she was glad now she hadn't.

She was rather sick of people asking about Broadmoor and what it was like inside, and all she could say was that her experience was limited to carol services at Christmas with her husband. There was usually a dig at what a scandal it was that people who'd done such wicked things should be allowed to live there in luxury at the public expense.

But escaping was different because local residents, without an alarm or siren to warn them, were usually unaware of an escape.

'Would they come down to the village?' John persisted.

'I don't think so. I think they'd be more likely to go over the other side of the hill,' she said, rather hoping he might now take the hint and go the same way.

'Would the attendants look for anyone in the village if they escaped?' John asked next.

'I expect they would look everywhere,' she said, grabbing one of the dogs by the collar, alarmed now that her visitor was showing no sign of leaving. 'Are you on holiday?'

John thought about this and nodded. 'Yes, I'm from Somerset.'

'How lovely,' said Mrs Spencer, rising for her chair. 'Now you will have to excuse me because there is a man coming from the village to deliver meat for the dogs.'

She put emphasis on the words man and dogs and to her relief her guest took a final slurp at his tea and also got up. Without a further word he lumbered to the door and was off down the drive, closing the gate carefully behind him at the end of the drive.

Mrs Spencer watched him go. Despite her directions about the path leading to the village and the bus, he turned back into the scrub and disappeared in seconds, away from the village and Broadmoor.

Then she turned to walk back into the hall, picked up the telephone and dialled the Broadmoor number.

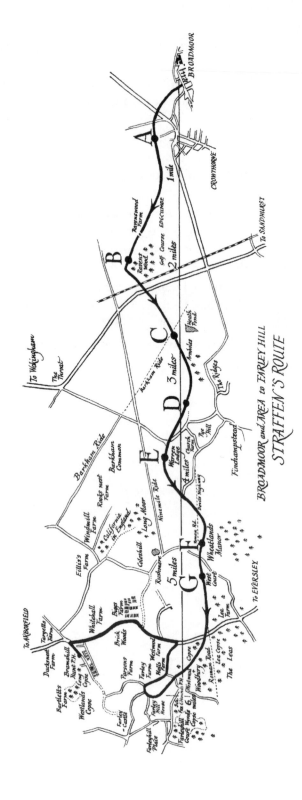

Diagram used in the trial of Straffen's route from Broadmoor to Farley Hill. *Trial of JT Straffen (Fairfield and Fullbrook)*

14

Back in the woods and alone again, John felt pleased with himself. That lady in the house had been completely fooled, a lady with four dogs and none of them suspected a thing. His suit and saying he was on holiday from Somerset did it. Still, he wasn't going to use the path to the village she suggested because if she was suspicious and told someone then they might find him on the path.

She said if anyone did escape from Broadmoor then they'd go in the opposite direction to town, so all he had to do was stick to the woods and then go straight into town and everything would be fine. The only trouble with the woods was they messed up his boots and tore at his jacket and trousers.

Once he heard some barking behind him and Straffen wondered if the lady had sent the dogs after him, but the barking soon faded. He wished he had a dog with him now because that would give him an excuse to be walking around the countryside like this.

Then the wood ran out and there was nothing for it but to take a deep breath and walk out into the street. Perhaps he'd meet a few of the local kiddies and they could chat a bit and he could tell them about his adventures, and show them all he wanted to do was talk and be friends. But there were no children around as they hadn't come out of school yet.

He turned into Crowthorne High Street. There were shops and people walking up and down, but nobody seemed to be looking at him.

He turned down another street and there up at the end were two men with bikes. He stopped dead in his tracks. They were looking down the street towards him and getting on their bikes.

John turned to retrace his steps and the moment he was around the corner he ran for it to the woods again.

He would stay in the woods now and only leave them when he was so far away from the men on bikes that it would be safe.

Safe to do what, though? It was always the same, wasn't it – whenever he wanted a bit of peace it was the attendants, the police, always someone telling him what to do.

After ten minutes he stopped running. He was getting out of breath and his work boots were too heavy and were starting to hurt his feet. He came out onto a golf course where it was easier to walk, but then up near the railway there were more men in uniform – it was hard to tell if they were from Broadmoor or the trains.

So it was back into the woods and popping out occasionally onto roads until a car came along, then it was back into the trees. Once he saw a man standing outside his house and John asked him the way to town. He thought if he said that then he wouldn't have to say what town. The man wouldn't look at him and John thought he might be blind, which was rather a relief. The man asked him if he was from these parts and John said he was from Bath when he meant to say Somerset, but the man had been to Bath and talked about how beautiful a city it was and had he visited the Roman Baths? John couldn't remember – he'd been swimming with the school but couldn't remember if the baths were Roman or not.

The man pointed the way to town but John took a different direction in case it was a trap, and anyway if the man was blind he probably didn't know what he was talking about.

Then after a bit he gave up the woods and walked the whole time on the road. It was getting warmer as the afternoon went on and it felt safe to stay on the roads. He was coming up a hill when he saw a pub at the top and four little girls sitting on the wall outside the pub. As he got nearer one of the girls was crying and she crossed the street to go into her house. The pub was called the Fox and Hounds and John could see he was in a village. It was not a big village and there were houses going up and down each side of the high street, with a school on the left and one or two cars parking outside a shop on the far right. The school gates were open and children were walking out to make their way home or were on bikes milling round in the road outside the entrance.

John slowed to a saunter so that he could take it all in. He walked past the pub. He nodded and smiled at the girls but they giggled and didn't take any notice of him. He then walked past a house beyond the pub that looked more like a skittles alley from the back. But as he passed the gate he saw a caravan parked in the drive and he was so thirsty he thought he might risk seeing if he could get a drink of water without having to ask anyone. The door of the caravan was open and he stepped inside. It was so cosy inside he wondered if he might live in there a few days and whether anyone would notice if they weren't using it. There was a bunk about the size of his bed in Broadmoor, and a small kitchen. The only thing it didn't have was water because when he turned on the tap at the small sink nothing happened.

Then he thought he could hear voices, women's voices, and the clink of china and cutlery like when he was an orderly in the dining hall at Broadmoor. From the caravan window he could see fields at the back of the garden and he thought he might be safer there.

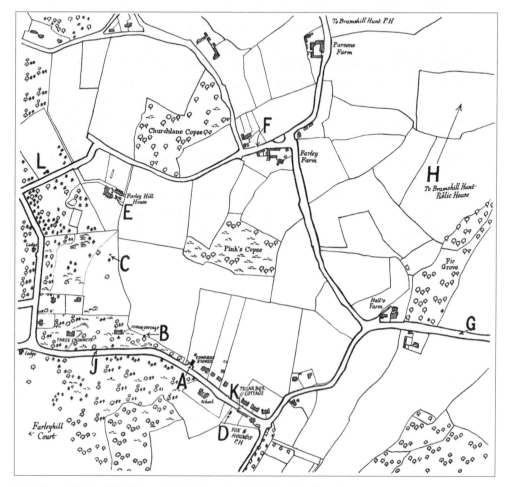

Trial Plan of Farley Hill village. *Trial of JT Straffen (Fairfield and Fullbrook)*

15

At four o'clock that afternoon Mrs Alice Sims was sitting in her back garden at Pillar Box Cottage in the village of Farley Hill. She was enjoying a cup of tea with her sister-in-law Mrs Huxtable, and because it was such a fine day they'd decided to take tea outside.

The beautiful weather reminded them that summer was around the corner and got them talking about holidays. Mrs Sims, her husband Roy and daughter Linda usually took their caravan down to Southsea where the sea was only a few hundred yards away from the site and Linda enjoyed playing on the pebble beach. But although the beach was clean and the shopping good in nearby Portsmouth, they were always glad to get back to Farley Hill where they knew everyone and things were, well, safe.

Just after 4 p.m., Linda pedalled her bike around the corner of the house on her return from school. Linda Bowyer was Alice Sims's daughter by her first marriage. She was nearly 6 years old now and enjoying her first years at the local village school. She threw the bike against the wall and came over to the grown-ups. 'Do you want a cup of tea, love?' asked her mother.

Linda nodded and sat down to tell them about her day. She hadn't quite got over the novelty of going to school and having a cup of tea like this made her feel even more grown up.

'Did you see your father on your way back from school? He's delivering some wood, he told me,' said Mrs Sims.

Linda shook her head.

'What you going to do now until tea?' asked her mother.

'Going up to play with the others,' replied Linda. That was what she and her friends usually did on a fine afternoon, bicycle up and down the high street before getting back home at 5 p.m. or so for tea.

With that Linda was up and gone, riding off on her bike. In a few minutes they saw her come round the corner, perform a couple of loops at the end of the drive and swoop off again.

As Mrs Sims poured them another cup of tea, her sister-in-law suddenly touched her on the arm. There was a man walking across the garden. They were so surprised they couldn't say anything. He was tall with a mass of blonde locks that need cutting. He wore, in Mrs Sims's words, a bluey-coloured suit.

'Who *is* he?' whispered Mrs Sims.

'He's come out of the caravan,' replied Mrs Huxtable.

The caravan was permanently parked down the side of the house, only visible around the corner to Mrs Huxtable.

As they watched he clambered over the fence at the bottom of the garden, looking up as he did so to see the two ladies for the first time. Without a nod or an excuse, he carried on into the field and was gone.

The ladies instinctively made their way to the caravan. 'There's nothing much in there to steal,' said Mrs Sims.

But once in the caravan it seemed obvious that the intruder was looking for no more than a drink. An empty cup sat on the draining board beside the small kitchen sink, and the tap remained turned on. Unfortunately for him the water wasn't connected and so he hadn't got his drink. Although it looked as if there had been a quick search through the kitchen cupboards nothing had been taken.

'If that's all he wanted I would have given him something to drink,' said Mrs Sims.

'He looked too smart for a tramp,' said Mrs Huxtable.

'Roy said they get a few like that at work, just turning up and asking for food or work.'

Mrs Huxtable went back to the door of the caravan and looked out. 'Still, he shouldn't just wander in like that and try to help himself. Do you think we ought to tell Roy?'

'I'll mention it when he gets back – he'll know what to do.'

As she said this, her husband Roy was driving his Morris van back from work to the village with a load of firewood in the back for his father. It was about quarter to five and he'd promised his father to let him have the wood that he'd collected after doing some clearing on the local estate where he worked as a manager.

Once in Farley Hill he stopped outside Edwards' Stores for cigarettes and an evening paper. He was only in there for a couple of minutes, but when he came out he saw Linda on her bike over the road.

'Have you had your tea?' he shouted over to her.

'No,' said Linda, at least that was what he thought she said because she was shaking her head.

'Is your mother in?' he asked.

This time Linda nodded.

'Is she getting the tea?'

Linda shook her head, and with that Roy got into his van and drove off.

Watching all this from Linda's side of the street was John Straffen.

16

After leaving the caravan John had been surprised to see the two ladies sitting in the garden. He decided to keep walking down their garden to look as normal as possible, then he climbed over the fence and walked along the back of the pub, as if he'd meant to do this all the time.

When John walked around to the front of the pub he found that the four girls had gone, and so he started back up the high street for the second time. He wanted a big bottle of lemonade like the sort he treated himself to in Bath after a long day working at Mr Byles's.

He'd only taken two steps when he saw one of the girls come out of the same entrance he'd just used to get into the caravan. She was on a bicycle and turned to ride up the street away from him. Several children were cycling up and down the street and she joined them, riding faster than them up the street and then wheeling back to join them. John walked slowly behind, past the school and then up towards the shop on the right. A man came out of the shop and started shouting something about tea across the street at her.

The girl didn't seem very interested in the man and made no effort to cross the road to join him. John felt a bit sorry for her. He'd like some tea as well. If he had some money he'd take both of them to the teashop and buy them a big tea with jam and scones and that sort of thing and he and the girl would become good friends.

Instead John let the van drive off and he followed the girl on her bike up the high street. Now she wasn't cycling very quickly and kept stopping. After a minute or two he went up to her from behind.

'Hello,' he said.

The girl turned around without saying anything back. She remembered him walking past her outside the pub, but before that she'd never seen him. She knew most people in the village, by sight anyway.

'I know that man you were just taking to,' he said. 'I've just met him in the shop.'

'That's my dad,' she said, more interested this time.

'What's your name?' he asked.

'Linda,' she replied.

'That's right,' said John. 'Your dad said take Linda to have some tea as your mum is busy and hasn't got tea yet.'

'She's with Mrs Huxtable,' said Linda.

'I'll take you for tea. I know a short-cut,' said John.

'Do you live around here?' asked Linda.

John thought about this for a moment. 'Just a few miles away,' he said, pointing in the direction he thought he'd come from that afternoon.

'Do you live in a big house?' Linda asked.

'A very big house,' said John. 'There are hundreds of us live there.'

'It sounds like a castle.'

'That's right – it's really hard to get into,' said John.

Again he cursed about not having any money otherwise he really could buy her tea.

'Do you like flowers? I know where you can pick them in the wood. You don't have to pay for them,' said John.

John pointed to the entrance to the fields at the side of the stores. 'This is the short-cut to the wood,' he said, and when they reached the field he offered to help her with her bike. But she was fussy about her bike and said she would push it. In the end John suggested she leave it in the field and they would come back for it when he'd shown her where to pick the flowers in the wood.

17

The grand title of nanny at Farley Hill House was given to the German twenty-two-year-old au pair, Miss Henrietta Jahn, who was sitting out on the front lawn of the house at ten to six on the fine evening, watching the two children of the Kenyon family play in front of her. This was the first afternoon of the year when this had been possible and was as much a relief to the children as it was for Henrietta after they'd been cooped up in the house for the winter.

The children's bedtime was six o'clock and she'd been keeping a careful eye on the time because if she overran 6 p.m. Mrs Kenyon would not be amused. Not that that happened very often because Henrietta was only too pleased to get the children to bed early and have a bit of a life of her own.

But at times like this Henrietta really enjoyed the job. She stretched her long legs out in front of her on the grass and watched the children run in and out of the bushes at the far end of the lawn. They'd be tired out at bedtime today and wouldn't need much in the way of reading or any other persuasion to go to sleep.

So it came as something of a shock to see the figure of a man lumbering through the bushes around the gardener's cottage. Visitors, whether friends or tradesmen, came up the drive at the front of the house rather than from the back through the woods.

This visitor hadn't seen her sitting on the lawn, so she stood up. When he finally saw her she called out, 'What is it you are wanting?'

'Drop of water, please,' he replied, although that's what she thought he said because he mumbled. Leaving the children playing where they were, she walked around to the kitchen door, or the tradesmen's door as Mrs Kenyon insisted on calling it, with their visitor. He didn't look at her, but kept his eyes to the ground. She fancied there was something rather Saxon about him: blonde hair a little too long that he kept pushing back, six foot tall and well built, coming out of the woods like a warrior frightening the women and children. The suit jacket was creased and the trousers wet at the knees as if he'd been kneeling on the ground.

Henrietta left him at the door without encouraging him to come into the kitchen, took a glass from the cupboard over the sink and filled it with water. She took it back to the door where he grabbed the glass and took a long gulp, almost choking as he did so. She noticed his fingernails were dirty and she didn't want him in the kitchen.

Leaving him at the door, Henrietta went back through the kitchen and into the sitting-room to consult with her mistress. Mrs Loyalty Kenyon was seated on the sofa reading a magazine.

'Excuse me, Mrs Kenyon,' said Henrietta.

Mrs Kenyon put her magazine on the coffee table in front of her. She didn't seem pleased to be interrupted. This was her hour before her husband returned from the office. Now in her mid-thirties she'd had to persuade her husband they needed a nanny for the children and the idea of an au pair had been something of a compromise. She felt rather pleased to have answered the advert in *The Lady* and to have appointed a German girl so soon after the war in an act of forgiveness.

'Yes, what is it, Henrietta?' she asked tersely.

'There's this man at the back door.'

'What sort of man?'

'He's asked for a glass of water, ma'am.'

Mrs Kenyon looked out of the sitting-room window as if she might see him roaming around the garden. Without their nanny the children were making too much noise. 'Is he trying to sell something?' she asked.

Henrietta gave a shrug and started to play with her plaits, always a sign of her not knowing quite what to do. 'All right,' said Mrs Kenyon, 'I'll come and see what he wants.'

When they got back to the kitchen John was still there in the back yard, but he had moved to the side of the house to watch the children play. He was smiling and waved encouragement to them. In return the children made even more noise, showing off as they played catch in the bushes. They knew the man was going to mean them going to bed late.

'Well, he looks respectable enough,' said Mrs Kenyon, looking out of the back door with Henrietta close behind. 'You'd better get him some tea.'

Mrs Kenyon then stepped out of the door. 'Would you like some tea, please?' she called.

John didn't move quickly – he was too engrossed in the game the children were playing. Then he came back to the door, nodded and looked uncertainly into the kitchen to see who exactly was there.

'Do you do a lot of walking?' Mrs Kenyon asked brightly while Henrietta put out a tray of tea things.

John nodded. 'Quite a lot today.'

'Where have you come from?'

John thought about this. 'About seven miles,' he replied. 'Do you have the evening paper by any chance?'

Mrs Kenyon went back to the sitting-room to retrieve the paper she'd bought earlier in Reading. She handed it to him through the door with the tray of tea. Their visitor took it from her and screwed up his eyes as he put his head close to the front page.

John drank his tea noisily. 'That's very nice tea,' he said.

'You sound like you're enjoying it,' said Mrs Kenyon.

'Do you have a wireless?' asked John.

'We do, but I'm afraid the battery's gone,' she said, considering this was one request too far. 'Thank you, Henrietta; you can get back to the children now. Mr Kenyon will be back home any minute now and I want the children in bed when he does.'

This was surely enough of a hint to encourage their guest to go. Even so he seemed reluctant to leave the paper, and turned to the back page to check what was in the stop press. Mrs Kenyon assumed he wanted the paper to find a local bed and breakfast. During the war she might have taken pity on him and offered a bed for the night, but not now.

Mrs Kenyon walked out of the door to check he did leave the premises. As he walked to the side of the house she heard Henrietta calling the children in from the garden and taking them upstairs to bed. But their visitor looked as if he expected them to be waiting for him as part of their game, to jump out of the bushes in the drive. When he realised they weren't there his pace increased, much to Mrs Kenyon's relief, and he loped off down the drive to the road, where he paused to take his bearings before setting off again with new purpose.

18

When Mr Sims got back to Pillar Box Cottage just after 6 p.m. he parked the van in front of the caravan in the drive and walked round to the back of the house. Alice Sims was in the kitchen washing up after her sister-in-law and getting the evening meal ready. 'Did you get the wood delivered?' she asked her husband.

'I had a cup of tea with Dad afterwards. That's why I'm a bit late,' replied Roy.

'Is Linda with you?'

'No, I saw her outside Edwards'. She was on her bike.'

'I think we'll start without her. She had a cup of tea here but nothing to eat.'

So the meal started, and ended, without Linda. This was not unusual in summer when Linda would skip her tea to go on playing with her friends, although she was aware of the rule that if you missed tea you went to bed hungry. But there was a lot to talk about this evening to put Linda out of mind for an hour or so.

'You'll never guess, but when we were having a cup of tea out at the back this afternoon a man came out of the caravan and walked down to the back of the garden, bold as brass,' said Alice.

Roy was spreading a thick slice of Mother's Pride with raspberry jam. 'What sort of man?' he asked.

'We'd never seen him before. A tall young man in his twenties. He'd been in the caravan. We reckoned he was looking for a drink.'

'He could have asked for a drink.'

'That's what we said. Anyway, he saw us and climbed over into the field at the back without saying a word.'

'He picked the wrong caravan for a drink.'

'Do you think we ought to lock it?'

Roy took a sip at his tea. 'We've never had to. What's it all coming to if you have to lock up a caravan sitting in your own drive?'

'We wondered if we ought to have told the police, but I said I'd ask you first.'

'As long as he didn't take anything. We have them wandering into work sometimes. Boss says leaves them alone if they're not doing any harm. What was he wearing?'

'A suit, a bit crumpled.'

'Demobbed, I expect. Given a cheap suit and told to get off out of it. I'm sorry for them really. Where are they going to get a job?'

Alice started gathering up the plates and cups and took another look at the clock. 'Still,' she said. 'He won't be bothering us again.'

19

Just before six o'clock Ernie Taylor was at the Farley Hill cricket ground when he heard someone whistling on the road that ran down the side of the ground. Ernie was a nursery hand and member of the club and he took it upon himself to keep an eye on the pitch. Like Henrietta up at Farley Hill House, he was taking advantage of the longer evenings to get outside and have a walk round the ground before he went home for his tea.

When the whistling persisted he looked up to see a man on the road beyond the fence. Ernie walked over to the fence and found him walking slowly along the lane, peering around as he did so as if he were looking for a house or turning. The man was tall, respectable enough, with a tanned face and rough hands suggesting he worked outside, the sort of person Ernie might have worked with himself at the nursery.

'Can I help you?' asked Ernie.

The man smiled, but it wasn't clear whether the smile was meant for him. 'Can you tell me where town is, please?' he asked, but Ernie only caught the word 'town' in the question.

'What town?' asked Ernie.

There was a mumbled but incoherent reply.

'Do you mean Wokingham?' asked Ernie, trying again. 'Well, if you go straight down the lane and right at the farm, and then left at the bottom of the hill you'll come onto the main road. You can get a bus there.'

The man thought about this for a while. The smile was still there, but the brow furrowed. 'How often do the buses go?' he asked.

Ernie explained and the man looked down at his wrist. 'Well, it's a quarter past six. All right, I've plenty of time,' he said and walked on down the lane.

Ernie looked on after him. He walked with a funny gait, as if his arms and legs were disconnected and not aiming in the same direction. That wasn't all that was funny about him: he'd looked at his wrist and told the time to the minute, but there was no watch on his wrist.

All this left John in something of a dilemma. He could be directed to all the bus stops in the area but he still didn't have a penny for the fare. He could try dodging the fare but he had had enough people chasing him already. He could walk it if necessary, but it would be quicker hitching. This was something he was quite used to doing in Bath, especially on cold and wet mornings when he didn't want to use his bike to cover the two miles out to the market garden at Bathampton. He wouldn't have any trouble now in his suit, not like Bath in his muddy work clothes and boots.

He was contemplating all this when a lorry came up behind him and he instinctively turned and stuck out a thumb. Lorries and vans were usually the best for lifts but the driver waved his hand at John as if he were too busy to think about lifts and drove on without slowing. Then a car appeared and to his amazement the car slowed in front of him and drew to a halt. It was a woman, and she was alone and smiling at him.

Mrs Dorothy Miles was driving through Farley Hill collecting dishes from local farms for a party to be put on by the Women's Institute later that evening, when about a couple of hundred yards from Simmonds' Farm she saw this suited young man hitching a lift. He looked a typical farmhand out for the evening, smartly dressed in a suit. Only when he got into the car did she notice the crumpled jacket, wet trousers and muddy shoes.

Mrs Miles asked where he wanted to go and he mumbled something about wanting to go to town. She wondered whether he might be drunk, or a foreigner perhaps, and told him she'd take him to the bus stop. It was nothing she couldn't handle, and they drove on in silence, her passenger taking quite a lot of interest in anyone in the road or any car they passed.

The bus stop was outside the Bramshill Hunt pub. As they approached the pub they could see uniformed officers of some sort a few hundred yards up the road. By now her passenger appeared to be on full alert, leaning forward to get a better view. 'Are they policemen?' he asked, or at least that was what she thought he said. 'What are they doing?'

'I really don't know,' replied Mrs Miles.

But they were now outside the pub, and her passenger clambered out without a further word. However, instead of walking to the bus stop he made a beeline for the pub and disappeared inside. By now Mrs Miles was so suspicious of this odd behaviour that she put the car into gear and drove straight up to the officers. They weren't policemen, but whatever they were she didn't hesitate in winding down her window and telling them exactly what she'd seen.

'That's him,' said one of them, and to a man they turned and ran back down the road towards the pub, so quickly that she remained seated in her car not sure whether she should follow them, stay where she was in case he reappeared, or move on home to Wokingham. The engine was still running and she noticed her hands were trembling. She wondered what he might have done. The man hadn't looked or sounded very bright and she guessed he was nothing more than a drunk – that's why he made for the pub. She took a final glance in the mirror, saw nothing, and drove on towards home.

Percy Horton and his three uniformed colleagues from Broadmoor Institution, posted on the Arborfield Road outside the Bramshill Hunt, were all male nurses and were stopping and warning traffic that one of their patients had escaped and could be dangerous. Passengers were taking it all calmly, although some were annoyed at the news and wondered how much it was costing the taxpayer to keep these people in luxury in Broadmoor without a guarantee they wouldn't escape.

They didn't have to hear much of Mrs Miles's description of her passenger, especially when she said she thought he was a foreigner with his odd speech, before they knew it was Straffen. A search of both bars of the pub quickly showed he wasn't there, and when asked customers confirmed a tall man having to stoop as he came through the bar had made no attempt to buy a drink but had passed through the garden door into the back of the pub.

The four officers tumbled out into the lane behind the pub looking more like the Keystone Cops than a force looking for an escaped killer. But here their luck changed, because the lane turned out to be a cul-de-sac, and as they rounded the corner whom should they find, holding audience with a group of eight or nine children, but the unmistakable figure of John Straffen.

Horton guessed that the moment Straffen saw them he would make off through the fields behind, and so he fanned off into a ploughed field to his left to try to cut him off. But it didn't take their quarry long to spot them and he immediately bolted through the field and into a wood. They tumbled after him, crashing through the undergrowth into the wood, where they came to a standstill, breathing heavily and cocking their heads to listen for him. When there wasn't a sound they concluded he'd hidden himself and soon found him crouching at the top of a bank like a cornered animal.

The struggle to capture Straffen was long and violent – even the four of them together could hardly contain him. The jacket started to rip as he struck out in all directions, biting any hand that tried to restrain him, kicking out at anything in uniform.

Then suddenly it was all over. The familiar grin was back on John's face and he started brushing the mud off his clothes.

'Are you coming quietly, John?' asked one of the officers, like something out of the movies John watched on Sunday afternoons in Bath.

'I'm hungry,' he replied.

They gave him a peppermint, and walked him back to the main road to their car, where they sat him between two of them in the back seat.

'Why were you with that group of kiddies, John – not up to your old tricks, I hope?' asked Tom Sands, one of the nurses, as they drove back to Broadmoor.

'No, no. I only escaped to show I'm innocent. I've given up crime,' was all John said, chewing his fingernails as he spoke.

He had been free for just over four hours.

1 No. 1 Camden Crescent, Bath, home of Brenda Goddard. *Author's collection*

2 Junction of Camden Crescent with Lansdown Road. *Author's collection*

3 Camden Crescent, east view. *Author's collection*

4 Brenda Goddard. *Real-Life Crimes Vol. 99*

5 The Private, murder scene behind Camden Crescent. *Author's collection*

7 No. 1 South View, Claremont, Bath, home of Cicely Batstone. *Author's collection*

8 Graves of Brenda Goddard and Cicely Batstone, Lockswood Cemetery, Bath. *Author's collection*

9 Mrs Violet Cowley, who spotted Straffen and Cicely Batstone shortly before the murder. *Real-Life Crimes Vol. 99*

10 Broadmoor Institution at the time of John Straffen's escape. *Trial of JT Straffen (Fairfield and Fullbrook)*

11 Inside Broadmoor – terrace and main block. *Trial of JT Straffen (Fairfield and Fullbrook)*

12 The Terrace, Men's Wing, Broadmoor. *Broadmoor (Ralph Partridge)*

13 The Front Gate, Broadmoor. *Broadmoor (Ralph Partridge)*

14 Refractory Block, Day Room, Broadmoor. *Broadmoor (Ralph Partridge)*

15 Linda Bowyer. *Trial of JT Straffen (Fairfield and Fullbrook)*

16 Police collect Linda Bowyer's bicycle and clothing for the trial. *Real-Life Crimes Vol. 99*

17 Mrs Pullen and Mrs Batstone
at Winchester for the trial.
Real-Life Crimes Vol. 99

18 Alice and Roy Sims, Linda
Bowyer's parents, arrive at court at
Winchester.

19 Sir Reginald Manningham–Buller, prosecuting counsel at Winchester. *Trial of JT Straffen (Fairfield and Fullbrook)*

20 Mr Henry Elam, defence counsel at the Winchester trial. *Trial of JT Straffen (Fairfield and Fullbrook)*

21 Mr Justice Cassels, presiding judge at Winchester. *Trial of JT
Straffen (Fairfield and Fullbrook)*

22 Mr Justice Cassels leaves court at the end of the first day of the trial
at Winchester. *A Man of Quality (I. Adamson)*

23 John Straffen is led away to start his life sentence. *Real-Life Crimes Vol. 99*

20

The news of John Straffen's escape from Broadmoor of course reached the police before the news of Linda Bowyer's disappearance. In fact the report to the police of Linda's vanishing came so late in the evening – at eleven o'clock without any satisfactory explanation of the delay – that the police started the search in the dark around Farley Hill and then had to abandon it in the early hours of the morning, resuming at dawn with dogs.

Daylight allowed them to spread the search into the fields and woods behind the high street and at 5.25 a.m. they found Linda's bicycle in an open field between the high street and Farley Hill House, and an hour later her body was found under an oak tree in the adjoining copse of trees. She'd been strangled. There was no sign of a struggle, and no sign of sexual assault. Nor had any attempt been made to hide either the bicycle or the body.

Chief Inspector Fred Francis, weary with lack of sleep after being up most of the night organising the search, was driven by DS Lawson to Broadmoor at 8 a.m. that morning to see John Straffen. Murders were never pleasant, but child murders he found particularly difficult. Mercifully they'd found Linda fairly quickly after daybreak, but then he'd had to call at Pillar Box Cottage to tell her parents and then face the prospect of interviewing the obvious suspect. Added to all this was the frustration of a prisoner being able to escape from Broadmoor with such apparent ease and with such devastating results. Why couldn't the locals be warned that someone like Straffen was on the loose?

While he was admitted pretty quickly at the main gates, it still took Inspector Francis some time to make his way through the various internal gates and doors, each of which had to be unlocked and then locked behind him, through to the impressive Victorian building where Straffen was being held in a side room. Francis, despite his seniority and length of service in the police force, had never been inside Broadmoor before and he was awed at the sheer size of the place, its daunting buildings looming like stately homes, and the manicured lawns with flower borders and mature trees leading onto gravel walkways.

But there wasn't much of the stately home where John Straffen had spent the night. Francis was steered to a room off the main hall where patients were secured if they'd become violent during a meal or recreation. John's torn jacket was thrown on the floor and he was fast asleep on a mattress on the floor, covered by a blanket. A cup of water sat on the floor beside him, and a police officer was stationed on the door outside.

'Would you like him woken, sir?' asked an attendant.

'Yes, please. Has anyone spoken to him since he was brought in?' asked Francis.

'No, sir. He hasn't even been brought any food. We thought we'd keep him fresh for you, sir, so to speak.'

The attendant bent down to the sleeping figure and gave him a couple of light slaps on the face to wake him up. John started slightly to see so many people in the room, and sat up on the mattress, rubbing his eyes and grabbing his cup of water to take a sip. He was wearing the remains of his ripped shirt, and there were clear signs on his face and chest of the struggle that took place on his arrest. His eyes hardly opened and his speech was slurred, as if he'd lost his teeth.

There was no chair or any other furniture in the room, so Francis squatted down beside him.

'We are police officers, John,' he said.

John nodded. 'That's right,' he said.

'We need to ask you some questions.'

'That's right,' John repeated.

'We want to ask you about your escape from here yesterday. Are you prepared to tell us what you did and where you went?'

Francis expected another monosyllabic reply, but instead John looked up and said, 'Yes. I jumped over the wall, went through some woods, across a lot of fields and a golf course. I had a cup of tea at a house, and then you lot caught me.'

Francis shifted his weight onto the other foot. 'Yes, yes, we know all that. The thing is, we need to know what else you did – and in particular whether you got up to any mischief?'

John leant back against the wall, cup in hand. 'I didn't kill her, if that's what you mean,' he said, his voice suddenly clearer after a drink of water.

There was a stunned silence in the room for a second or two, broken only by the slurp of John's lips as he took another sip of water.

Francis leaned a little closer. 'What do you mean, John – you didn't kill her?'

'That's right,' said John.

'But we haven't said anyone's been killed, or injured, or attacked.'

John smiled and looked up at Francis. 'I know what you policemen are. I know I killed two little children, but I did not kill the little girl.'

Francis looked up at Detective Sergeant Lawson. 'What do you know about a little girl being killed, John?' he asked.

'I did not kill her,' repeated John.

Sergeant Lawson now knelt down beside John in a scene that was beginning to resemble a wartime military field hospital. 'The thing is, John, a little girl was in fact killed quite close to where you were arrested,' he said.

John now turned to him. 'Well, all I can say is I did not kill the little girl with the bicycle.'

'What do you know about a girl with a bicycle?' asked Francis.

'I did not kill her,' repeated John.

This line of questioning was not getting them further, although his replies had already brought them miles in seconds. John was visibly relaxing at having got these rehearsed lines off his chest. 'So why did you escape, John?' asked Francis.

This time he did not hesitate with an answer. 'I did it to prove I could be outside without killing little children,' he replied.

Francis got to his feet. 'All right, John, that's all for the moment. We are going to have a little break now to give you the chance to have a wash and something to eat, if that's okay with our friends here?' He looked over to the Broadmoor staff, who gave him a nod. Francis and Lawson were shown into a room with a desk and telephone and asked if they might be brought a cup of tea.

'Well, Arthur, we're never going to get an admission out of him, but he's said enough to hang himself. We've just got to be sure no one has spoken to him overnight to give him the chance of knowing about the murder,' said Francis.

As they drank their tea, Francis put a call through to Bath police and spoke to Detective Inspector Coles. 'I know you dealt with Straffen on the other two children,' he said. 'He's escaped here from Broadmoor and it looks like he's killed another one.'

Lawson could hear the groans coming from the other end of the phone. 'The thing is,' added Francis, 'he's not going to come across on this one, but I wondered how much it was worth persevering. You didn't seem to have much trouble.'

'Let him make a written statement. He likes that,' advised Coles. 'But he won't say any more now. His memory's good – he'll give every detail except for the one bit you want. That's the way he works. There'll be ten minutes missing there somewhere in his story, you can bet on it.'

The two officers went back to their prisoner's small room armed with paper and a pencil. 'Better get his clothes off to forensics,' said Francis on the way, 'and a sample of whatever's under his fingernails as this is a strangling case.'

But when they asked John if he had any objection against scrapings being taken from beneath his nails, he said, 'You're cunning, aren't you? You're looking for flesh – they did that to me before – but you'll be unlucky this time.' Sure enough, when he held out his hands like a schoolboy having his hands inspected before lunch, the nails were bitten back to the quick.

21

Next morning, on 2 May 1952, John Straffen appeared before Reading Magistrates' Court. The courtroom was crowded and when his name was called all eyes turned to the tall, stumbling figure coming up the steps, looking more like someone pulled out of a pub brawl than anything more sinister. While the crumpled jacket and torn shirt had been replaced with a smart sports jacket and clean shirt, the black eye and bruises to the head showed that he had not come quietly. He blinked, looked around the court as if he was hoping to recognise someone, and then stooped, head down, with his hands on the front of the dock. He remained handcuffed to one of the two warders standing each side of him.

Inspector Brazell for the prosecution told the court that after he'd been charged, John replied, 'I did not kill her; that's a frame-up, that is.'

As he said it, John nodded.

The clerk of the court turned to the prisoner. 'Do you wish to be represented, Mr Straffen?'

'Yes,' came the faint reply.

'Do you want a legal certificate?'

'Yes.'

'Do you understand what I am saying?' the clerk asked.

There was a pause while a good number in the court half expected the prisoner to say no. But he nodded a yes, letting his mouth fall open.

'Have you got a solicitor or will you leave it to the magistrates to choose for you?'

John looked around the court again as if he might spot a solicitor. Despite there being a good number of them sitting on the benches in front of him waiting to represent their clients, he turned back to the court. 'The magistrates,' he said.

The case was then adjourned and John taken back down to the cells to be given a list by the court office of local solicitors who undertook crime work. He said he didn't mind whom he had on the list. So a few phone calls were made by the office and a solicitor found from a local Reading firm.

The court then reassembled and John's new legal representative had his chance to address the court.

'Your worships, while my client is not making any application for bail, there is of course the question of his being returned to Broadmoor rather than being remanded to a normal prison. Your worships will be aware that an order was made by Mr Justice Oliver as recently as October 1951 at the Taunton Assize that my client be detained at Broadmoor and it is my submission that my client be remanded there until his trial.'

The chairman of the bench didn't look convinced. 'The point is, if Broadmoor Institution has once allowed your client to escape then what is to stop him doing it again? Naturally we don't want to act in excess of our duty, and it seems we have no precedent to follow as this situation is unprecedented – no patient has ever escaped from Broadmoor and been charged with an offence committed while free. What are your views on this, Inspector?' he asked turning to the prosecution.

'I share your concerns, sir, over the question of security. In normal circumstances the court would be asked for a remand in custody, and in normal circumstances it would always be granted. But there is nothing very normal about this case, and I would respectfully suggest that the court's first concern will be to protect the public. The learned judge making his order in October could not have foreseen the apparent ease with which the prisoner escaped from the institution and the possible consequences. The court will also be aware of the public outcry that has followed the escape and how vulnerable the public feels,' said Inspector Brazell, summing up what most people felt about the whole business.

The three magistrates retired to their room at the back of the court for a cup of tea and a digestive biscuit. 'The trouble here is that we are damned if we do, damned if we don't,' said the chairman to his two colleagues, tapping his biscuit on his saucer.

'Well,' said one of his colleagues, 'I'd rather risk infringing a judge's order than face any more of the hysteria coming from the press. And I'd have to agree that half of the inmates of Broadmoor are perfectly sane and enjoying the high life when they should be locked up in a proper prison. Our friend in the dock out there seems remarkably unconcerned by the whole thing. I'd like to wipe that smile off his face. I suggest Brixton or Wandsworth for his remand. He won't get out of there in a hurry.'

They filed back into court for a third time to await those heavy footsteps coming up the dock steps.

'Well, Straffen, we've decided to adjourn your case for a week to allow the necessary papers to be prepared for committal proceedings to an assize court,' announced the chairman. 'Meanwhile you will not be returned to Broadmoor, but remanded to Brixton Prison to await your trial. We appreciate there is an order made by the learned judge at Taunton last October, but it is in the public interest that you be held safely as it appears your present institution is unable to do this. What I have said is not to prejudice the very serious offence for which you are yet to be tried, and we shall be notifying Mr Justice Oliver on the action we have taken. No doubt your solicitor, now you have one, will advise you on any appropriate action to take if you wish to challenge our decision here this morning.'

The bench retired, relieved to have got rid of their troublesome prisoner, for a week anyway.

John was taken down to the police cells and given a mug of tea. He was fussy about his tea and gave directions to the police as to the strength and amount of milk he wanted. After a brief word with his solicitor, who said he would see him during the week at Brixton to take full instructions, John was placed in the back of a police car, still in handcuffs, and driven up to London.

For the second time, at the age of 21, John Straffen was to be tried for his life.

Daily Mirror

THURS
MAY 1
1952

1½d

No. 15,074

FORWARD
WITH THE
PEOPLE

Registered at G.P.O. as a Newspaper.

WHY?

John Straffen, 22, the man who escaped from Broadmoor in daylight.

WHY was Broadmoor escape so easy?

WHY no alarm of 'lunatic at large'?

"DAILY MIRROR" Reporters · Crowthorne, Berks, Wednesday.

FOR four hours yesterday, while children played in the sunshine and picked bluebells in the woods, a lunatic roamed the countryside around here after escaping from Broadmoor Criminal Lunatic Asylum.

During those four hours, a child disappeared. Today they found her body, about 500 yards from her home. She had been murdered—strangled.

WHY no action after warnings by staff?

Police are now trying to find out who committed the murder. Tonight, they sent a report to the Director of Public Prosecutions. Meanwhile angry and frightened parents in the scattered farms and villages around Broadmoor were asking these questions:

● WHY had the escaped lunatic, John Straffen, been given the position of a "trusted orderly" only six months after he was found unfit to plead to a charge of murdering two little girls at Bath ?

● WHY was he able to get a suit of ordinary clothes and wear it under his institution overalls ?

● WHY was he able to acquire and conceal a blanket-rope ?

● WHY was he able to fling this over a 16ft. wall and climb over, in daylight, without being seen ?

● WHY were three large disinfectant drums allowed to be left near the wall, so that they could be used as "steps" to aid his escape ?

● WHY did he have time to strip off his overalls and get clean away before the alarm was raised ? AND ABOVE ALL—

● WHY is the scattered population around Broadmoor not warned when a lunatic—who may be a dangerous man—escapes ?

This last question is the subject of a Parliamentary query tabled tonight by the M.P. for the Broadmoor district.

Local parents are saying that if such a warning had been given, the murdered child, five-year-old Linda Bowyer, would not have been allowed out of her home at Farley Hill—seven miles from here—to play.

And, whoever killed her, SHE WOULD HAVE BEEN ALIVE TODAY.

In Farley Hill, village of 200 people, an emergency meeting of the local Parents' Association being called to demand that some system of siren

Continued on Back Page

TWINS DON'T THRILL ME, SAYS INGRID

By DONALD ZEC

FILM star Ingrid Bergman expects twins in June, according to X-rays ordered by her husband, Roberto Rossellini. Ingrid is "a little frightened."

If one of the twins is a girl she will be called "Isabella." They have not yet decided on a boy's name.

On the phone from Rome last night, thirty-seven-year-old Ingrid told me: "Roberto took me to a doctor on Monday. I felt somehow that a double event was a possibility. X-rays were taken and the photos did indicate twins.

She expects them to arrive at the end of this month or early in June.

"It was quite a shock at first," she said, laughing, "but now I am getting used to the idea. I cannot say I am thrilled—twins are quite a thing to handle.

"Roberto is delighted," she added. "So I am glad for his sake."

Pretty Low

When I last spoke to Miss Bergman in Rome a few weeks ago she fell ill.

"I am still feeling pretty low," she said, "although everything is as normal as you can expect—with twins ! "

The couple have one other child, Robertino, aged two. Miss Bergman also has a thirteen-year-old daughter, Pia, by her first husband, Dr. Lindstrom.

Hottest day ends in storm

STORMS hit many parts of Britain last night after the hottest day since last September.

Hottest spot was London, with a temperature of 77 degrees recorded at Kensington Palace—13 degrees above Tuesday's highest.

And in many parts of South-East England and the Midlands it was the same warm story, with temperatures high in the 70's.

Then came the thunderstorms. A plane was struck by lightning near Gatwick, Surrey, but was undamaged.

Heavy rain doused Torquay and Bournemouth. Outlook today: Cooler.

Linda Bowyer (above), the five-year-old girl who was found strangled a few miles from Broadmoor.

Her body was discovered, after an all-night search, near the bicycle she was riding when she left her home at Farley Hill.

Right: Yesterday's picture of Linda's mother, Mrs. Alice Sims, and her stepfather, Mr. Roy Sims, with their son Gary, three months old.

Front Page *Daily Mirror* 1 May 1952.

22

Meanwhile the papers were asking why an escape from Broadmoor was apparently so easy. The *Daily Mirror*'s single headline 'WHY?' was typical: why was escape so easy; why weren't the angry and frightened parents in the scattered farms and villages around Broadmoor given any warning; why was John Straffen able to wear his civilian clothes and wander around the area unrecognised by local residents?

The question of why the population was not warned was the subject of a question in the House of Commons by the MP for Wokingham, who suggested that a siren should be installed at Broadmoor and that if there had been a warning then Linda Bowyer would still be alive.

The Prison Officers' Association issued a statement saying the staff at Broadmoor had frequently expressed concern that Broadmoor was regarded as a hospital while ignoring the dangerous types inside and the security systems. A memorandum had been sent to the institution regretting the transfer of responsibility from the Home Office to the Ministry of Health. This was another chapter in the ongoing debate since 1949 when the Criminal Justice Act transferred control of the Broadmoor Criminal Lunatic Asylum into the hands of the Ministry of Health, when it became the Broadmoor Institution and criminal lunatics were no longer treated as criminals but patients in need of medical support.

On 29 May the *Daily Express* published an article headed 'Broadmoor Officers Tell Bad to Worse Story'. According to the report, attendants were saying it was not their fault and that serious incidents were necessary to show that security no longer existed in Broadmoor, that they'd warned the authorities they couldn't run the institution like an ordinary mental hospital, and that the policy now was to abandon the wearing of uniforms because they annoyed the patients. Winston Churchill, the Prime Minister, was so concerned about the article he wrote to his Minister of Health for an explanation. Iain Macleod wrote back denying that the Board of Control had made any changes to threaten security, and claiming that this was the Prison Officers' Association trying to prevent the blame for the escape attaching to an individual member of their union, and to strengthen their case in a current wage claim.

The situation was not helped by those who remembered the escape from Broadmoor of James Edward Allen, who strangled 17-month-old Kathleen Lucy on 19 June 1937 and then ten years later in 1947 escaped from Broadmoor dressed as a cleric, to be dubbed the 'Mad Parson'. Allen was at large for two years before he was recaptured, but he was eventually released from Broadmoor in September 1951, less than a year before John Straffen's escape.

In Crowthorne, where John had wandered freely in his blue suit accepting the hospitality of Mrs Spencer, 2,000 people packed the public square in the high street for a protest meeting. Half the town turned up with villagers from miles around, and passed a resolution for a public warning system, better watch over patients, and for control of Broadmoor to be handed back to the Home Office. However the vicar of Crowthorne, the Reverend Nuger, warned the meeting that the first thing any patient who escaped would do would be to break into a house and steal a suit – so they were asking for greater danger.

The Superintendant of Broadmoor, Dr Stanley Hopwood, resigned and went into retirement with a CBE after a distinguished career in which he transformed Broadmoor from an asylum into something more like a proper mental hospital. Among his reforms was the introduction of parole within the confines of the hospital allowing free movement within the walls as the highest privilege. He also introduced insulin and ECT as treatments and appointed psychotherapists as staff. During this period attendants in the hospital came to be called nurses and prisoners called patients, as well as the management of the institution passing from the Home Office to the Board of Control at the institute. This was why there was a strong feeling in certain quarters that following the escape, management should pass back to the Home Office. He was also the author of a book titled *Child Murder and Insanity*, which must have given him food for thought in his retirement.

It became clear that with the public outcry the government would have to act and act quickly. In a Cabinet meeting on 6 May 1952 Iain Macleod presented an internal report from the Board of Control at Broadmoor. The report said that the job of cleaning the surgery building was one of the first jobs given to new patients after a period of investigation and observation. The situation had been complicated by building work going on in that area with workmen coming in and out of the door to the yard from where John Straffen had escaped. Straffen had behaved well in his short stay at Broadmoor and his only spell outside the main buildings had been in a high-walled kitchen garden. The Board laid the blame for the escape fair and square on attendant Cash for failing to keep his charge under direct supervision. The Board denied the allegation by the Prison Officers' Association that security had suffered with the transfer of Broadmoor from the Home Office to the Ministry of Health and the Broadmoor Board of Control. The report made the point that a good proportion of the staff was over sixty, and Mr Cash himself sixty-eight. The only reservation about installing a siren was that when there was an escape a large number of the staff was sent out in pursuit. If a siren sounded, the patients would know someone had escaped and that there were fewer staff on duty in the institution.

Clearly a full and independent enquiry would be now needed and the Cabinet asked the Minister of Health to tell the House of Commons that afternoon that he intended to do this. Next day, at a further Cabinet meeting, Iain Macleod outlined the proposed make up of the committee of enquiry. This was approved and the minister asked to proceed.

Then, on 8 June, Churchill wrote again to Iain Macleod asking him not to discuss, in public at least, which government department should have control over Broadmoor.

When the internal report was presented by the Minister of Health on 20 June 1952, he quickly denied there had been any relaxation of security rules since 1949 and rejected any suggestion that control should be handed back to the Home Office. He also, perhaps uncharitably, laid most of the blame at the feet of the hapless attendant Mr Cash who had been in charge of the two-man working party on the day, and who had allowed John Straffen to go out into the yard to shake his duster unsupervised. The Board's disciplinary enquiry, he reported, established neglect of duty by the attendant and recommended a severe reprimand. A more severe

Subject File

Criminal Proceedings.

PRIME MINISTER'S
PERSONAL MINUTE

SERIAL No. M. 316/52

MINISTER OF HEALTH

You should not commit yourself in public upon the
question of whether Broadmoor etc. should be under the
Home Office or the Ministry of Health until the matter
has been considered by the Cabinet. Every Department
naturally tries to keep as wide a sphere as possible
for itself. But this Departmental esprit de corps should
not be allowed to prejudice the decision to which we must
come in due course.

I gather that the precautions at Broadmoor are
being appreciably strengthened. This is to the good but
in itself implies a criticism upon the system which had
been allowed to develop. Where murderers are concerned the
safety of the public, especially in the neighbourhood,
must claim priority.

W. S. C.

8 June, 1952

Churchill's Minute 8 June 1952. *The National Archives*

penalty could have been recommended, he said, but the attendant had a nine-years' unblemished record. Criminal proceedings could have been taken against an attendant for negligence but it was decided this wasn't justified in this case.

A full enquiry was immediately announced by the Minister of Health, to be conducted by five commissioners with a free hand to look at the escape and the general question of warning local residents if there was an escape.

The enquiry committee, which reported on 17 June, found that before the war no one escaped from Broadmoor between 1932 and 1940, but that in the next nine years there were six escapes, and then between 1 January 1950 and 29 April 1952 there had been another six escapes. But the committee felt that security had not been compromised by treatment for patients rather than concentrating solely on the detention of prisoners. However, many of the locks on the premises were old and had been opened by prisoners who had made keys. There was a staff shortage and the quality of the staff was lacking, which was due to staff being paid insufficiently compared to other mental institutions. The last security rules were printed in 1908 and were now out of print.

One crucial issue was allowing patients to wear ordinary clothes, and while the committee didn't want to stop this, it was suggested that when a patient was at work and wearing distinctive work clothes, then access to his ordinary civilian suit should be prevented by locking the cupboard or box in which the suit was kept.

Then came the recommendation that a siren be sounded as soon as an escape was discovered and this should be connected to local police stations and schools, with the press and the BBC being notified so that they could play their part in warning the public. The siren would be a call for all working parties to return and for all off-duty staff to report in for work at soon as possible.

For Churchill and his government, Straffen's escape, which they regarded as one waiting to happen, had opened a number of political issues bubbling underneath the surface. The Prison Officers' Association was unhappy with its role inside Broadmoor and one of its members getting the blame was the last straw; Dr Hopwood had resigned as Superintendent of the Institution, doing the honourable thing after years of bringing real progress to Broadmoor; the local residents were up in arms over their and their children's vulnerability without proper alarm systems; and Churchill's own government departments were starting to bicker over who should have final control over Broadmoor.

While the trial of John Straffen was never going to be the solution to all these problems, Churchill must have hoped that there would be sufficient bloodletting to calm everyone down and to put Straffen back into Broadmoor under proper supervision and security. But the trial was to throw up as many questions as answers, with Churchill himself unsure as to what had happened in the trial and having to write to his Home Secretary for an explanation.

23

On 1 July 1952 John Straffen's trial for the murder of Linda Bowyer opened at the Castle, Winchester. It was assumed that he would be held unfit to plead and the whole matter would be sewn up by lunchtime, with a flea in the ear of the Broadmoor authorities for letting him escape.

So it came as a complete surprise when John mumbled a couple of words to the clerk of the court when asked how he pleaded to the murder of Linda Bowyer. As he did so he looked over uncertainly to his solicitor, who nodded encouragement, and he articulated 'Not guilty' at the second attempt. In other words, he was to be tried as a person of sound mind, despite the fact that another court had found him unfit to plead to murder only eight months ago and sent him to Broadmoor.

Leading counsel for the prosecution was Mr Reginald Manningham-Buller QC, an MP and Solicitor General. He was a man who did not suffer fools gladly and he was known among his colleagues as 'Bullying-Manners' because of his aggressive style of examining in court. He was a large man, someone with whom you would not choose to pick a fight in or out of court.

Against him, as counsel for the defendant, was a very different character, Mr Henry Elam, a barrister not drawn from the ranks of Queen's Counsel – surprising for such a high-profile case – tall and lean, a man preferring to persuade rather than cajole.

Presiding over the trial was Mr Justice Cassels, a man much more to everyone's image of a judge with his bushy eyebrows and air of gravitas. On the opening day of the assize he carried a nosegay of flowers from his official car to the court door in a tradition going back centuries to when judges needed protection against the stench of the courts, dressed in scarlet robes and full-length wig, with the power to send a prisoner to the gallows or to an institution like Broadmoor for as so long as it pleased his King or Queen.

But behind this daunting exterior was a former prisoner of the Japanese in the Second World War, when Harold Cassels worked on the Burma railway and had learnt fluent Japanese. As a result he had sympathy for the underdog. Once, when trying two young defendants for stealing two cigarette lighters they found in the street, he admitted he might well have kept them himself. On another occasion he was trying a pop star's lighting engineer for cultivating cannabis, and in giving him a conditional discharge admitted there was something rather touchingly amateurish about two tiny plants in a trough on a bed.

Cassels showed a similar humanity earlier in his career as a barrister, when he was prosecuting a man for stealing a motorcycle. Upon discovering the man had no defence barrister, Cassels offered his own services, and proceeded to comprehensively destroy his own arguments, at the end of which the magistrate commended 'both counsel' for being most helpful and dismissed the case.

Always a hands-on judge, Cassels once heard a case where the accused claimed to have been injured by police handcuffs. Cassels asked to try them on himself to help the jury, only to find the police didn't have a key. He had to adjourn the trial to eat his lunch in the handcuffs until a key was found.

Manningham-Buller opened the case for the prosecution with a seventy-five-minute address outlining to the jury the case he intended to present to them and the nine witnesses he would call to help him do it.

After lunch a legal argument followed as a result of the prosecution wanting to introduce evidence of the two Bath murders. This ran against the general legal principle that similar fact evidence should not be introduced in a trial as it was likely to prejudice the case against the defendant. In this case it would follow that Straffen's admissions to the Bath murders could show that the circumstances of the murders were very similar to the present murder of Linda Bowyer. However, similar fact evidence had already been used in notorious cases like that of George Joseph Smith and the 'Brides in the Bath' murders to establish a pattern in the events surrounding the murders.

Here Mr Elam, for the defence, argued that introducing such evidence would prejudice his client and tip the scales against him. After a discussion in the absence of the jury, the judge decided that the evidence should be admitted, and anyway it was probable that every member of the jury would know of Straffen's record from the publicity surrounding the Bath murders eight months ago.

At about four o'clock, while this application to bring in evidence of the Bath murders was still going on, the judge brought the jury back into court to tell them they wouldn't be needed again that day and that they could go home to be back at 10.30 a.m. next morning.

But before releasing them he gave the jury a stern warning. 'Do not discuss this case with anybody else, or allow anybody else to discuss it with you, and if you should see anything in the press regarding certain submissions which have been made to the court, do not bother your heads with them. You see, you have taken an oath, and you are the twelve people, the only twelve people in this wide world, who have taken an oath with regard to this case, to try it according to the evidence that you will hear in court, and it would not be right or just that you should try it according to something else. So will you just keep your minds from anything anybody wishes to say to you, and from anything you may see in the newspapers, until the case is over, so that you may come into the jury box with fresh minds.'

There is something almost liturgical about these warnings to a jury at the end of the first day of a long trial, warnings that they might bring down the wrath of God if they disobeyed, but meanwhile they should go in peace while knowing in their hearts their fate if they do not heed the warning.

So the second major surprise of the trial came the next morning when the judge finally appeared after a one-hour delay and, stony faced and with eyebrows twitching, addressed the jury. 'Members of the jury, you will remember last night I warned you very earnestly that you should not discuss this case with anybody. Owing to the alleged conduct of one of your number, which has been reported to the court, I am compelled very reluctantly, and with great regret, to discharge you from further dealing with this case. I must request you to remain in court until it is possible for that matter to be properly investigated, and the court has indicated the course that it proposes to take, and it may be that some of you will be required in another court for service upon the jury. There you, I am afraid, have to cease to act as a jury in this case.'

The jury then filed out of court wondering who among their twelve was the Judas, and it was not until lunch that they found out. They were brought back into court, this time not to sit in the jury box but to be lined up in front of the judge. The police then ushered in a witness from Southsea who had attended a meeting on the previous evening where one of the jurors had told the audience about his day in court on the Straffen case, that in his opinion Straffen was innocent and, if that wasn't enough, it was one of the prosecution witnesses who had committed the murder.

The juror was then identified by the witness and told by the judge to remain in the court building for the rest of the trial, and to think not only about the amount of wasted public money, but also about having to drag Linda Bowyer's parents back into court for the ordeal of giving evidence all over again.

24

With the first jury now dismissed and the offending juror somewhere in the castle contemplating his fate for the duration of the trial, a new jury was sworn in. This time the jury had two women and ten men, perhaps with the hope the female influence would reduce the risk of the males misbehaving.

The clerk of the court then told the jury that John Straffen had been charged with wilful murder and had pleaded not guilty. The prisoner stood at the front of the dock between two warders, his head lolling forward and his chin nearly touching his chest. Some members of the jury were gazing at him, wondering whether he was going to pass out in the heat or even have a fit. Then he sat back on the dock bench in the same position for ten minutes or so, before suddenly coming back to life, looking around him and at the guards, muttering something to them and nodding his head.

The Solicitor General then gathered his considerable bulk, flapped the tails of his gown a couple of times, adjusted the wig on his perspiring forehead, and rose to the unenviable task of repeating his opening address from the day before. The temperature outside was reaching the eighties (°F) and Mr Manningham-Buller was clad in a thick wool suit, waistcoat, black gown, stiff collar and horsehair wig. He paused occasionally to mop his forehead. He could have cheerfully strangled the juror who'd made him repeat his speech and then re-examine his witnesses.

In the circumstances he managed to reduce the length of his speech by twenty-five minutes. He reminded the jury that they had to be satisfied beyond reasonable doubt that the accused was guilty of murdering Linda Bowyer. He said that from the outset he should tell them he would not be able to produce any witnesses who had actually seen Straffen in the company of Linda Bowyer.

After outlining the witnesses and evidence the jury was about to hear, he turned to the question of the accused's sanity. At this John came out his trance and looked up. Counsel said that in considering verdicts of guilty or not guilty, the jury could consider a verdict of guilty but insane. But he added that everyone is presumed sane and responsible for his actions, and that this applies even to someone who had escaped from Broadmoor. It is for the defence to put forward the defence of insanity, and if they do then the burden of proof is not so heavy as that of the prosecution establishing guilt. The defence would have to show that Straffen was suffering from a disease of the mind and did not know what he was doing or did not know he was doing wrong. The prosecution would wait and see if that defence was put forward.

Mr Herbert Noyce, a surveyor from Berkshire County Council, was called first to the witness stand and he produced several diagrams. Exhibit 1 showed in detail the immediate area in Farley Hill where the murder took place (see page 80), to include the point where Linda's bicycle was found and the spot where her body was found nearby. The diagram also showed the jury Linda's home at Pillar Box Cottage and Edwards' Stores. A smaller-scale diagram (see page 76) was also introduced showing the route taken by John Straffen from Broadmoor to the village of Farley Hill, and then the route out of Farley Hill towards the Bramshill Hunt pub where he was left to catch a bus and caught by the Broadmoor attendants instead.

The court took a bit of time considering the diagrams, which had a habit of rolling up with a zip as the members of the jury did their best to cope with the catalogue of detail being thrown at them by counsel. But as diagrams went they were professionally produced, helpful with their markings describing the terrain and features of the countryside, and not the sort of thing often produced by the articled clerk in the solicitor's office in the weeks running up to the trial.

After a couple of police officers gave their evidence about finding Linda Bowyer's body, the pathologist Dr Robert Teare confirmed that death was by strangulation and, when asked, said that this would have taken about fifteen to thirty seconds, and that the victim would not have been able to scream once the hands had touched her throat.

After the German nanny at Farley Hill House and her mistress Mrs Kenyon had given their evidence, describing how John had been given water, tea and biscuits, the evening paper, and would have been given access to the radio had it not been for a flat battery, a rather sheepish Mr Oliver Cash was called.

Mr Cash gave his evidence in a flat monotone and at the age of sixty-eight looked as if he'd much prefer not to be in court that morning nor indeed anywhere in the area of Broadmoor.

He confirmed he was supervising the prisoner in the surgery buildings at Broadmoor when he escaped. 'Straffen came and asked my permission to shake the duster outside the door in the adjoining yard,' he said.

'That meant going out of the building into the yard?' asked Mr Hutchinson, junior counsel for the prosecution, giving his leading counsel a chance to perspire seated next to him.

'Yes, just outside the door.'

'What did you say when he asked to do that?'

'Yes, all right.'

'Did you see him again that afternoon after that?'

'I did not.'

'Did you go out in the yard after you let him go out?'

'I did, about two minutes later.'

'And was he not in that yard?'

'He was missing,' said Cash impassively.

'Does the yard adjoin the wall of the institution?'

'Yes, the outside wall of the institution.'

'Was there any way in which a person could have climbed that wall and got over it?'

Mr Cash paused a moment to check he'd been asked such a silly question. 'Yes, the way he did it. There were some empty disinfectant tins standing outside and close to a small lean-to shed.'

'It would have been possible by getting on to those tins to have got on to the roof of the lean-to shed?'

'Yes, quite easy.'

'And from there to the top of the wall?'

'Yes.'

'You then gave the alarm?'

'Yes.'

The judge interrupted here to ask, 'How high is the lean-to shed?'

'It has a sloping roof, my lord. The highest part is about eight feet six inches, within about eighteen inches from the top of the wall.'

'So it is about a ten-foot wall?'

'Yes, about that, my lord.'

Mr Elam then got to his feet for a short cross-examination. 'Mr Cash, how many patients were you looking after at the time?'

'Two.'

'Do you always look after two, or do you sometimes look after one, or sometimes look after more?'

'Sometimes one, and sometimes any number up to half a dozen.'

'What sort of patients are they?' asked Mr Elam finally.

'Lunatics,' replied Mr Cash tersely, summing up the way he felt about people asking him questions about the whole affair.

When Mrs Alice Sims, Linda's mother, was called to give her evidence, she looked like a woman living a nightmare – having lost her daughter in the tragedy, she now had to give the same evidence twice in as many days.

She confirmed she lived at Pillar Box Cottage, Farley Hill, and on 29 April was at the back of the house having a cup of tea with her sister-in-law. At about 4.30 p.m. they saw a man walk uninvited from their caravan parked at the side of the house. He seemed surprised to see the two women as he left. As usual Linda came back from school and went back out on her cycle to ride up and down the high street. That was the last time Mrs Sims had seen her daughter. Linda's bedtime was 7.30 to 8.00 p.m.

Her husband Roy was next. He said he was an estate worker and that on 29 April he'd been out in his Morris van. He stopped at Edwards' Stores for a few minutes and when he came out he saw Linda on her bicycle on the other side of the street. He asked her if her mother was getting the tea and she said no, and with that he drove back home down the high street.

Mr Alfred Barker lived opposite the school in the high street and that afternoon he was picking some chives in the ditch outside his house. He saw a man come across the road and thought he was going to speak to him, but instead the man kept walking and disappeared into the gateway of the house next door. That man was the prisoner now in the dock. The last he saw of him, he was loitering by a gateway in the high street, and then moving back down the street in the opposite direction.

As counsel admitted in his opening speech, none of the prosecution witnesses so far had actually seen John Straffen and Linda Bowyer together

118

at the same time: there was plenty of evidence to show Linda was cycling around the high street with her friends after school, even shouting across the street to her father at one stage, and plenty of evidence to show John Straffen ploughing his way in and out of people's gardens from the high street, but no one was saying they saw them together.

John had had time to think about what exactly he was going to say to the police overnight at Broadmoor, and it remained to be seen if he would stick to his usual tactics of telling the truth as much as possible without actually incriminating himself. The tactics had worked well for the first murder, but whether it would succeed this time remained to be seen, especially as it couldn't be taken as a foregone conclusion that what he had said at first to the police after his recapture could be used as evidence at all.

25

hief Inspector Francis was called next by the prosecution. He was just explaining to the court that he went to Broadmoor to interview Straffen after his recapture in order to take a statement, when he was stopped midflow by Mr Elam objecting to his evidence.

The jury was sent out by the judge. Mr Elam, looking more like a benign schoolteacher than ever, stood up to say that John Straffen, after being returned to Broadmoor, was in his view in custody and therefore should have been cautioned by the police before answering important questions likely to incriminate him. Mr Elam went on to say that the Judges' Rules could not have foreseen this sort of situation where the prisoner was not in a police station or prison. It was the Judges' Rules that lay down that a person in custody had to be cautioned before what he said to the police was admitted as evidence in court.

Mr Justice Cassels listened carefully to all this. 'I am afraid I must differ from you on this point, Mr Elam. I do not think it means that at all; I think it means "in custody" as it's understood by everybody, namely police custody. That is to say, where a man is taken to the police station and is held there, he is not there by invitation. When you take this present case, he was in an institution.'

'Yes, my lord,' said Mr Elam, already realising he wasn't going to get far with this. 'There are staff called nurses and the inmates are called patients, but the fact remains he is in custody there by the order of the learned judge.'

'That means he shall be detained as a Broadmoor patient – it is not custody for this purpose. If it were, and an offence had been committed and the police wanted to make enquiries, then the moment they put their noses inside Broadmoor then they couldn't ask any patient a single question without first cautioning him,' said the judge.

Mr Elam saw that it was hopeless. He made a parting shot, saying, 'I submit this is not the same as putting questions to an ordinary patient.'

The jury was recalled and Inspector Francis was allowed to tell the court that once inside Straffen's room and asked if he'd been up to any mischief, John replied that he did not kill the little girl, without any prompting as to what he might have done in the way of mischief. When told that in fact a little girl was killed quite near to where he was arrested, Straffen added he did not kill the little girl with the bicycle, despite no mention of a bicycle.

Straffen then made a written statement, said Inspector Francis, this time after a caution. He made the statement fluently and without any difficulty in giving an account of his movements. At the end he didn't wish to add or subtract anything, simply saying, 'No, that's it.'

The clerk then read the statement out to the court:

Yesterday I went to the surgery to work. I did one room and then I got a duster and went to Mr Cash and asked him if I could go out and shake the duster. I was out about two minutes and then another patient came out and asked me if I had finished shaking the duster. I said, 'I have just finished off now,' and he went back in. I then climbed the roof and then I jumped over the wall and ran down towards the road.

I climbed over a fence into some woods. I went through the woods and saw a road and I ran down. I got down the bottom of the road. I crossed the road and went down a lane. I got to the end of the lane. I saw a woman outside her house. I asked her for a cup of water. She gave me a cup of water and a cup of tea. When I had drunk that I asked her which way I could get through the woods to the village. She told me.

I went through the woods and came out near a school. I think it is Crowthorne. I walked down the street and crossed the road and turned down another road. There was a shoe shop near the corner. I went down this road and saw two men on bikes. They turned round and came back and I dived through the woods.

I came from the woods on to a golf course. I climbed up towards the railway lines. I saw two staff at the far end and then I climbed over the wire and ran through some people's gardens. I then crossed the road into some more woods. I then walked right through the woods. Then I walked up a path in the woods. I saw some people by a house near the main road. I crossed the main road into some more woods. I saw a man near a house; I think he was blind. I asked him which way I could get through the woods. He told me to go on one way but I went the opposite way.

After about two or three minutes I came to another path. I came to a private house. I walked through the grounds. I climbed into a field. I kept to the fields for a long time after that. I then came to a main road near a village. I went into another field and kept in the field for about two minutes. I then walked up the hill. I saw a pub on top of the hill. I saw about four little girls talking in the road not far from the pub. One of the little girls ran into her house crying, the other two went towards the pub. The other one went back to her house and when I looked back she had a bike and was riding up behind me. I heard a man, I think he was from the shop, ask her if her mother was home. I think she said, 'Yes.' The man then got into a van which was parked outside the shop. I then walked straight along the road. I turned round again. The girl was not there at all.

I then went to a house along the road past the shop. I went to the house. I saw a woman and two children outside on the lawn. I put my hand up and she came over to me. I asked her for a drink of water. She gave me a drop of water. Another woman in the house asked me if I would like a cup of tea. I said 'Yes'. She gave me a pot of tea, milk, sugar and biscuits and brought me out a newspaper. She then left me to read my newspaper and drink my tea. When I had finished I took all the stuff back inside the house and asked if she had a wireless. She told me she had one but the battery had gone. I then closed the door and left.

I then went on towards the road away from the shop and turned right. I got about ten to fifteen yards. I saw a man in a field and asked him where was the nearest town. He told me about six miles. I asked him what time the buses were running, and he told me, 'There's one about ten past seven that night.' I told him I had got plenty of time. I then walked down the road which he told me. I met two more people and asked them which was the quickest way to the bus stop. They told me to take the left road; there were two roads where I was speaking to them. I went down the left-hand road, then I saw a man on a bike. I said, 'Good afternoon' to him, and he said the same to me. I walked down towards the main road. A lorry came along. I tried to get a lift. He did not stop. After about five minutes another car came down. I put up my hand and she stopped. She asked me which way I was going. I said, 'Towards the town.' She gave me a lift and I was speaking to her in the car. She asked me if I was a foreigner. I said 'No.' I told her I came from Hampshire and told her I lived in Winchester. I did not speak no more. After that she dropped me by a pub and I got out. She told me a bus would come along.

She drove on. I saw her stop again, and I saw her speak to the staff, so I ran through the pub. I came out on a field. I saw some children in the field so I climbed through into the army barracks. I came back into the same field again. I saw the children again. I looked towards the main road. The children got frightened, they wondered what it was all about, so I climbed into another field then and ran. I saw the staff coming from the other fields. I climbed through another wire fence then which led into some woods. After about two minutes I climbed up a bank and hid. The staff then came and caught me.

I have been shown a photograph by the police officer of a little girl and that is a photo of the little girl who I saw with the bike near the pub and who followed me up the road.

The clerk confirmed the statement was signed and had been read over to the defendant and dated 30 April 1952.

There was an impressed silence in court when everyone wondered how a person as apparently vacant as the prisoner was able to make such a detailed statement, where every step in this odyssey had been recalled in perfect detail. Looking at him in the dock, his shoulders slumped and his head back down on his chest, with his mouth hanging open, their next thought was whether the police had written it for him, or at least helped him along.

John had even put in seeing the girl, and admitting she was the one in the police photo. For the first time in the proceedings the shadow of a doubt crept into their minds – was the whole thing quite as straightforward as the prosecution suggested? After all, the prosecution admitted from the start that no one had actually seen Linda Bowyer in the company of John Straffen, and there seemed to be enough people around in that high street to see most of what had been going on that afternoon.

Inspector Francis, watching all this as he waited to resume his evidence, thought of what Inspector Coles had said to him from Bath over the telephone: Straffen will give you everything you need to know, except the vital ten minutes.

Francis was asked a few more questions about precisely what he'd said to Straffen before he started denying killing a little girl and referring to the bicycle. Some of the staff at Broadmoor were then called to make sure they hadn't mentioned the killing overnight before Straffen was questioned.

Then it was the turn again of Sergeant Lawson, adding that with his son he'd timed walking between some of the vital points on the diagram. For example, it had taken them two minutes fifty-six seconds to walk from where Linda's body was found to where her bicycle was found; one minute fifty-six seconds to walk from the bicycle to the road outside Edwards' Stores; and six minutes twenty seconds in total to walk from Edwards' Stores up to the garden of Farley Hill House via the spots where the body and bicycle were found.

A local window cleaner was called to say that in the late afternoon he'd been called to Lady Palmer's at the Dower House to remove a television aerial for her butler. On his way up the high street he'd noticed Linda Bowyer on her bicycle playing with some other children. He'd particularly remembered her because she'd been in his way and he'd practically had to get off his bike to get past her. When he'd returned from the job at Lady Palmer's he'd not seen Linda, but he had seen three of the other children sitting out in front of the Fox and Hounds reading a book.

Mrs Molly Chadwick had been down to the Fox and Hounds herself to visit relatives who were staying at the pub. She'd left at 5.40 p.m. to walk back down the high street and she seemed to have met and chatted to half the village in doing so: Mr Walmsley outside his house, Mrs Hutchinson and her daughter outside her bungalow next to Edwards' Stores, Mr Finch actually in the copse of trees next to Edwards' Stores, then Miss Deane coming from the bus stop, and finally young Michael May giving a ride to Anne Hutchinson on his bike.

In short, she'd met just about everyone that afternoon except Linda Bowyer and John Straffen.

26

Mrs Chadwick was the last of the prosecution witnesses relating to the Linda Bowyer murder. The prosecution then moved on to the murders of Brenda Goddard and Cicely Batstone in Bath as the court had agreed to hear the evidence.

After a Bath police photographer gave his evidence, Inspector Tom Coles was sworn in and confirmed he had been in charge of the Bath enquiry into Brenda Goddard's murder behind Camden Crescent. He said he'd known Brenda quite well because he lived near the family.

'I have also known John Straffen since he was 7 years old,' he added, opening a manila file and leaning it on the stand. 'He was born at Bordon, Hampshire and at the age of 2 went with his parents to India where his father served in the army. In 1938 they came back to live in Bath, but in June 1940 John at the age of 10 was certified as a mental defective under the Education Act 1921. In 1939 he had stolen a purse from a little girl who'd gone out shopping for her mother and was put on probation for two years. Then in June 1940 he was before the Bath Magistrates for breach of the probation and sent to a home for mentally defective children in Sambourne, Warwickshire; then he was transferred to Besford Court, Worcester, from where he was discharged in March 1946 at the age of 16. He then came back to Bath and was employed as an errand boy. In September 1947 he was charged with housebreaking and asked for thirteen other similar cases to be taken into account.

'In July 1947 he assaulted a 13-year-old girl in an allotment by placing a hand over her mouth and saying, "What would you do if I killed you? I have done it before." The girl escaped without injury. Then in September of the same year he killed five fowls in Bath by wringing their necks and leaving the carcases in the fowl run. He also said he had committed a number of sexual offences, but I cannot find any truth in this.'

Mr Manningham-Buller rustled his papers and flapped the tails of his gown. 'Did Dr Leitch, the medical officer at Bristol Prison, then give evidence to the court at Bath?'

Inspector Coles took a sip of water from a glass handed to him by one of the ushers. 'That's right,' he said, looking down at his notes. 'The accused was certified and sent to Hortham Colony, Almondsbury, a home for mental defectives. He escaped from there twice. On one occasion he was violent when arrested by the police. But he was granted licence on 14 April 1951 when he came back to Bath and lived with his parents. He found employment as a garden labourer in a market garden just outside the city. He followed employment quite normally, as far as we know.'

Now it was the Solicitor General's turn to have a sip of water, turning to a fresh sheet of papers as he did so. 'And were you in charge of the investigation of the second murder, of Cicely Batstone on 15 July 1951?'

'I was, my lord,' said Tom Coles looking over to the judge. 'Straffen appeared at Taunton Assizes before Mr Justice Oliver. The only evidence taken was from Dr Parkes, then the medical officer at Horfield Prison, and as a result Straffen was found unfit to plead on the direction of his lordship. He was ordered to be detained in safe custody at His Majesty's pleasure, and that order is still in operation.'

'When you were dealing with the housebreaking offences he committed in September 1947 and asked for them to be taken into account, what sort of recollection did he have of these offences?' asked Mr Manningham-Buller.

'He had a very clear recollection, in that he was able to point out the houses that he'd entered even though we'd had no complaint from the occupiers of the houses in question. Furthermore he was able to show us not only where the houses were but where he'd disposed of the stolen property by hiding it nearby, and in many cases the property was recovered as a result of his information.'

Mr Justice Cassels interrupted to ask, 'Did he say anything to you at that time in relation to these offences to indicate he knew it to be wrong for him to steal?'

'He appeared to realise the seriousness of his offences, my lord,' Tom Coles replied, and with his evidence completed he stepped down from the witness stand.

For the second time in the trial the mother of a murdered daughter was asked to give evidence. A year ago almost to the day Brenda Goddard had been murdered behind Camden Crescent and this had not been long enough to remove the pain lines written into Mrs Doris Pullen's face. She told the court that a year ago she lived at No. 1 Camden Crescent and on Sunday 15 July she had last seen Brenda at ten minutes to two, but couldn't find her at ten past two. As she searched she saw a man crossing the road coming from the copse.

'Would you recognise that man again?' asked junior counsel for the prosecution, giving his leader a rest.

'Yes, indeed I would,' she replied quickly.

'Do you see him here?'

'Yes, I see him,' said Mrs Pullen looking over to the dock.

'Is that man Straffen?'

'Yes, definitely. He went right across the road, up Lansdown towards St Stephen's Church.'

John Straffen sat in the dock, head down on his chest, staring at his hands and turning them over occasionally, as if he were ticking them off for doing what they'd done without his permission. When he heard his name mentioned he opened his mouth as though to speak and then closed it again. A moment later he yawned and stretched himself.

A warder bent forward and asked if he'd like a drink. 'No, I'm all right,' he replied, now staring at the witness.

Mr Elam got to his feet and confirmed he did not wish to put any questions to Mrs Pullen who, after being thanked by the judge for coming to court to give what must be very difficult evidence, stepped out of the witness stand to cross the court to join Mrs Batstone.

Mrs Daisy Batstone was called next. She was a slight figure in NHS glasses, with hair pulled straight back and fastened behind her head. Mrs Batstone gave her short evidence in a whisper, emphasising the tragedy of what she was saying to the court.

'I live at No. 1 South View, Camden Road, Bath,' she said, barely audible.

'On 8 August 1951, when did you last see your daughter?' asked counsel.

'She went out of my house at quarter to two. She was going to the cinema – it was children's day. I communicated with the police, and on the following morning I went with Inspector Coles to the Royal United Hospital, Bath, and there indentified her body.'

The brevity of her stark evidence suddenly brought home to everyone in the court that they were now hearing of the death of a third little girl from the third mother. The judge felt that whatever he said to her would be insufficient, but nevertheless he thanked her, and she crossed the court to rejoin Mrs Pullen.

It was getting near the lunch adjournment, and the judge felt they'd probably had enough for one morning, so he welcomed the chance to give the families a break for an hour and a quarter. This in turn gave the judge time to get back into his car and return to his lodging house for a quick lunch and a talk to his clerk about the plans for the rest of the week, before clambering back into the car for the return trip. For the barristers it was a sandwich in the court's robing room or a trip over the road for lunch in a hotel, then phoning into chambers to speak to the clerk with time estimates as to how long the trial was likely to take. Solicitors might lunch with their counsel to discuss progress generally, or repair to a local hostelry with the newspaper.

For the witnesses and families, without any catering facilities on the premises, it was a matter of doing the best they could to find a local café or pub.

Mrs Pullen and Mrs Batstone had travelled down to Winchester together from Bath – leaving their husbands at work – and they had put up in a local bed and breakfast. The two women had struck up a friendship. Mr and Mrs Sims, with less of a journey than the others, chose to go home at the end of the court day. They all agreed that the friendship that had grown between the three bereaved families was about the only positive thing to have come out of the whole tragedy. For the Pullens and Batstones in Bath, the relief six months ago of not having to give evidence at the Taunton Assize was eclipsed by the shock and disbelief of seeing the newspapers announce the escape from Broadmoor followed by another murder.

But the biggest ordeal for the three mothers was coming face to face with the killer of their daughters and, instead of the image of the monster that had haunted them day and night since the murders, finding someone who was only half there. Straffen was much younger than the figure in their nightmares, a man whose actions resembled those of a child. He probably spoke the same language as their daughters, he would play the same games as them and he was someone whom a daughter would trust enough to explore The Private with, accompany to the cinema on the other side of town, or abandon her bicycle to search together for bluebells, despite mother saying they never should.

27

The feeling of new momentum in the proceedings was spurred by the appearance of Mrs Violet Cowley, who was not only married to a Bath police officer but who just happened to be walking her dog at eight in the evening of 8 August 1951, past the field known as the Tumps in Bloomfield Road, when she saw a man in the field with a young girl aged about 9.

Mrs Cowley was an attractive woman wearing a high-peaked hat with a feather pointing up at the roof of the court. Counsel on both sides straightened their backs as she was sworn in, and the judge smiled at her before she gave her evidence rather than after when he usually thanked the witnesses.

She was asked first by Manningham-Buller to describe the man she'd seen in the field.

'He was about six feet tall; he was wearing a navy-blue suit, he had light-coloured hair, almost blonde, and no hat,' she replied. 'They walked to the end of the footpath, turned to the right and went up the slope into the field behind the hedge. They were walking side by side, but not hand in hand.'

You could almost see the court thinking no wonder she was married to a police officer, judging by the way she gave such a detailed and precise description – after all, she had only been walking her dog.

'Do you often see people in that field?' asked counsel.

'No, it is very rare. So much so that I spoke to my husband, who is a police officer. The next morning he was called out on special duty at 7 a.m. and I went with him and Sergeant Evans to Bloomfield Road and showed them where I had seen these people.'

Mrs Cowley said that later she had picked out John Straffen in an identity parade at Bath Police Station.

As Mrs Cowley gave the court one last brilliant smile, it became obvious that Straffen had made very little effort to hide himself or Cicely Batstone as they moved around Bath, from the bus conductor who knew him from work, to Mrs Cowley walking her dog and the courting couple who came within feet of them lying in the field.

DC Smith now took the stand to describe finding Cicely's body, right along the hedge in the corner of the field. He described how he and DC Cowley went up to the flat at 2 Fountain Buildings and arrested John Straffen, and then brought him down to the police station.

DC Smith then produced his notebook and, after receiving permission to use it in court, went on to say, 'Straffen told me that he went to the Forum first and then the Scala. I talked to him about the film at the Scala and it was obvious to me that he had seen it, as I had also seen that particular picture. He said that when he and the little girl came out of the Scala they walked through some new houses and up into Englishcombe, walked along and through a gate into a field, along by a hedge, and the little girl said she was tired and lay down. He came out and left her. Later he added that she was dead under the hedge when he left her.'

At this point Smithie paused, and put down his notebook to look up at the court. 'Straffen seemed to find this all amusing, and Sergeant Evans asked him if he realised the serious position he was in. Straffen replied that the girl was dead but we could not prove he did it. He then laughed. He then added there was another couple in the field.'

Next up was DS Albert Foster from New Scotland Yard, looking more urbane than his Bath colleagues, with an estuary accent in contrast to their West Country burr.

It was left to the clerk of the court to read out the statement taken from John Straffen by DS Foster. After dealing with the cinemas and walking up to the field afterwards with the girl, whom Straffen described as a bright little girl wearing a grey jumper and a blue-coloured frock, the clerk continued, 'She was tired and laid on the grass. It was turning towards evening. She was asleep when I left her, right near the hedge, facing the slope, lying on her side. After leaving her I bought some fish and chips at a shop near the old bridge, near the traffic lights, and I think it was about a quarter past ten when I got home. In the field there was a bit of a struggle. She went limp. I was holding her in front by the neck. A few years ago I had a breakdown.'

DS Foster said that Straffen had said to him, after he made his statement, 'The other little girl, I did her the same. You have got no witness. I did not feel sorry. I forgot about it. I had no feeling about it.'

DS Foster added that at times they had difficulty in understanding what John Straffen was saying, but at other times there was no such difficulty. On the whole he made his statements in quite a sensible fashion.

The last two witnesses for the prosecution were the police doctors who had seen the bodies of the girls on site in Bath and then examined them later at hospital. Dr Charles Gibson, as police surgeon to Bath police, was first. Dr Gibson was a distinguished, white-haired figure in middle age with a soft Irish accent. He wore a dark suit and tie, and looked quite at home in court. While in the corridor of the court waiting to be called he chain-smoked cigarettes.

In the case of Brenda Goddard, Dr Gibson confirmed that he'd examined her body in Bath Royal United Hospital and had found abrasions on the right and left side of the neck. There were also lacerations at the back of her scalp consistent with the child's head being struck against a stone, but while that injury might have stunned her it could not have caused her death.

'What was cause of death?' asked counsel.

'Asphyxia, due to manual strangulation.'

'Was there any sexual interference with this little girl?'

'None at all.'

Comparing the two cases of Brenda Goddard and Cicely Batstone, asked counsel, had their deaths been caused in exactly the same fashion by manual strangulation?

'Yes,' replied Dr Gibson, who went on to confirm that in both cases there had been no sexual interference nor had there been any attempt to hide the bodies.

Dr Robert Teare had been sitting in court listening to Dr Gibson, and when he was called he confirmed he had dealt in a similar way with Linda Bowyer's body. He agreed there were many similarities between the deaths of the three girls.

'In the case of Linda Bowyer, there was no apparent motive, was there?' asked counsel.

'None.'

'Was there any evidence of a struggle?'

'I could see none.'

'And no attempt to conceal the body?'

'None at all.'

'Would concealment have been fairly easy in that case?'

'Yes.'

'Was there any feature about the death of Linda Bowyer which impressed itself upon your mind?'

'Yes, at the time I was struck by the precision with which this child's death appeared to have been caused. It struck me that the pressure on the neck was determined and applied at exactly the right points, as if by a person with some experience of this method of killing.'

'The injuries which she sustained were very local in character, were they not?'

'They were.'

'Do you attach any significance to that?'

'They were in contrast to the exaggerated amount of bruising and external injury which one commonly sees in cases of strangulation, even in young children.'

'From the knowledge you now possess of the death of Cicely Batstone, was the same feature apparent there?'

'Yes, but more marked than in the case of Linda Bowyer.'

Mr Elam for the defence had only one question. 'Are you satisfied, Dr Teare, that those little girls were complete strangers to Straffen?'

'From what I have read, I do believe so,' Dr Teare replied, and he looked a little surprised that this was the only question he was going to get. Mr Elam asked the judge if the two doctors could be released to return to their professional duties, and they left with thanks from the judge.

Now it was the turn of the defence to try to work a miracle.

28

It's the unenviable task in a long trial like this for the defence counsel to get up at the conclusion of the prosecution case, when the evidence for the prosecution seems overwhelming and repugnant, and to try to put together some sort of defence. For Mr Elam this was made all the harder because his client was a mental defective and unsuitable to put in the witness box and, if he got it wrong, the only penalty fixed by law was death by hanging.

So it was left to Mr Elam to fill the role of conjurer, to flatter the jury and to see what crumbs he could find under the table to save his client.

The first thing that had struck the jury about Mr Elam was how nice he looked and sounded, without the blustering manner of his opponent for the prosecution. He was always polite and he had an understanding smile, occasionally turning to his solicitor, who in turn spoke to their client in the dock without receiving more than a nod or shake of the head in response.

Mr Elam stretched himself to his full height, as if this might give him an inch more authority in what he was about to say to the jury in his opening address. He looked down at the notes he had written up the previous evening in his hotel.

'Members of the jury, I am instructed to defend this man Straffen,' he started without great enthusiasm. 'This is, you may think, an interesting case, a famous case, an important case, both from the public point of view and from Straffen's point of view.'

At the mention of his name, John looked over to his counsel with that half smile everyone in court now knew.

'And you are, if I may say so without any fulsome flattery, most important people – the verdict is and will be yours and nobody else's, yours alone,' announced Mr Elam solemnly, hoping he didn't sound as if he was flattering to deceive.

But the flattery was at least making the jury look interested.

'This is a tragic case, whichever way you look at it,' Mr Elam continued. 'You have seen – and what a pathetic sight it was – the mothers of these little girls and their relations come into the witness box. It is also a tragic case for John Thomas Straffen whom you are trying for the wilful murder of Linda Bowyer, and whom as recently as 17 October last year was found unfit to plead by a prison doctor, and sent at Taunton Assizes by Mr Justice Oliver to be detained in Broadmoor Institution until His Majesty's pleasure be known. That order committing him to Broadmoor is still in force.'

Mr Elam continued on this theme by suggesting that if the accused was not John Thomas Straffen, with all the surrounding infamy of his escape and previous murders in Bath, then the evidence presented against him would be pretty thin. 'Or are they seeking to make him a scapegoat for what has happened; a scapegoat from Broadmoor?'

Without criticising the judge's decision to include evidence of the Bath murders, Mr Elam pointed out that in most cases they, as a jury, would never hear anything about what had happened before the crimes, until after a conviction. Nor did he like his client being asked by the police whether he'd been up to any 'mischief' while he was out of Broadmoor. This was a man who had been certified twice and had a mental age of 9: what sort of answer were they going to get?

'You may think it was the answer they got: "I did not kill her." What is Straffen going to think in Broadmoor, where he has been detained or put inside as being unfit to plead? Unfit to plead on what? On a charge of murdering two little girls.'

Mr Elam also pointed out that the prosecution witnesses were contradictory about the times of sightings of Straffen and Linda in the high street at Farley Hill, and also in their descriptions of the directions in which the two of them were going.

Mr Elam then announced that he was calling two reliable witnesses, a Mrs Tanner and her brother Mr Crouch, who lived near Edwards' Stores and who had made immediate statements to the police, saying that they had heard a scream at about quarter to seven in the evening – so much so that they ran out into the road to see if there was anything they could do about it. The scream came from the direction in which Linda Bowyer was found. This was the time that Straffen was getting a lift from Mrs Miles and was taken down to the Bramshill Hunt pub.

Mr Elam then turned to the question of his client giving evidence. The court had heard his lengthy statement being read out, and the fact that he'd twice been certified and once sent to Broadmoor as being unfit to plead, meant that he would not be helping the court by giving evidence. If he did, the spectacle of a mental defective giving evidence would be pathetic and tragic, and one that he was not asking them to witness.

The defence would also be producing Dr Parkes, upon whose evidence Straffen was sent to Broadmoor last October because he was not fit to enter a plea. They would also hear from Dr Williams, who was supervising Straffen while he was in Broadmoor.

Mrs Alice Tanner was then called as the first defence witness and she confirmed that she actually lived at Edwards' Stores on the Farley Hill high street.

'I used to keep the shop,' she said, 'but I sold the business to Mr Edwards and I kept the house. I remember the day of Linda Bowyer's death as a very hot day.'

'In the late afternoon of that day were you in your house?' asked counsel.

'At five o'clock we were having tea in the kitchen-dining room. I stayed in the room until quarter to seven or seven o'clock, when I went into the garden at the back of the stores. My husband and my brother were in the garden with me. There is a field at the side of us; from our back kitchen door we look right across the field.'

'Between the time you had tea and the time you went into the garden, in which part of the house were you?' asked counsel.

'I was in the kitchen the whole time, ironing.'

'Can you see from the kitchen into the field?'

'From the kitchen door; if I went to the door, I could.'

'During the time you were in the kitchen, did you happen to see anyone in that field?'

'No one at all.'

'You went into the garden at quarter to seven; while you were in the garden did you notice anything?'

'What I did notice was what I heard – the three of us – a scream, which I naturally thought were some pigs.'

'Did it seem to be near you, or far away from you?'

'Quite close.'

'From which direction did it appear to come?'

'It came from the coppice, which is at the side of the road.'

'Is that the coppice lying up at the side of Tudor Cottage?'

'Yes.'

'What did you do when you heard that scream?'

'We waited a minute or two, and as we did not hear any more we thought we would walk out on the road and see what happened. We wondered if a child had been knocked down. A lorry passed very soon after, almost as soon as we went out, and it was going in the direction of Arborfield. We were more concerned about finding out if it was a child or somebody who had been knocked down. We looked the other way and we saw nobody; there was not a soul on the road either way.'

Counsel paused a moment to take a carafe of water and pour himself a glass. 'During the time you were in the garden, did you see anyone come through the gap by the side of Edwards' Stores into that field?'

'No.'

'If someone had done so, would it have been possible for you to see them?'

'We could not have avoided seeing them.'

'Did you make a statement to the police on the next day after Linda Bowyer's death?'

'I think it was made the day after because I was away.'

'At any rate, it was within a day or two?'

'Yes.'

'Is your husband fit to come to this court?'

'No. He suffers from his heart.'

Mr Elam thanked his witness and handed her over to the prosecution.

Mr Manningham-Buller got to his feet and looked like a man not to be messed with when it came to any threat to the prosecution case.

'Mrs Tanner, you were busy ironing that afternoon, were you?' he started. 'Were you looking out to see who was passing up and down the road?'

'I am afraid not,' she replied.

'And unless you go to the kitchen door, you cannot look out across the field?'

'If I am sitting at the kitchen table I can look across the field.'

'If the door is open?'

'Yes; the door was open. I was ironing and it was very hot.'

'How far had you got into the garden before you heard this scream – about ten yards?'

'Yes, I should think not more than that.'

'Were your husband and your brother both gardening?' asked counsel, in a tone suggesting that anyone doing their own gardening could never be completely reliable.

'Yes, we were looking across the field and the scream was to our left. I said that sounds like a pig. Just at the time there was a lorry passing, but I don't know if it had pigs on it.'

'But your brother said "It sounds like a kiddy"?' asked counsel, not happy using the vernacular.

'Yes, we both thought it came from the road but there was no one about.'

Once again Mr Elam had to face a witness, his own witness this time, who was not being helpful to his case. 'Wherever it was, are you sure there was a scream?' Mr Elam asked, re-examining his witness with a note of desperation.

'I am perfectly sure of that,' said Mrs Tanner, trying to make up lost ground.

'And so you told the police?' asked Mr Elam, in a last throw to show the court how concerned his witness was about the scream.

Mrs Tanner drew herself up in the box and pushed out her chest. 'I told the police because I thought it was my duty to do so.'

As Mrs Tanner left the stand Mr Elam was in half a mind to scrap calling her brother, but then decided he could hardly do more damage.

Fred Crouch confirmed he also lived at Edwards' Stores and he remembered that he was in the garden at quarter to seven on the day of Linda Bowyer's death, when he heard the scream from a child, although his sister thought it was pigs.

'When you heard the scream, what did you do?' asked Mr Elam.

'We hesitated, and I made a remark that it was a child's scream. We stood there a minute, and then we went out to the road, because I thought a van which had passed had knocked down a child.'

The Solicitor General rose slowly from his seat, which he let snap shut behind him. 'It was a squeal, not a scream, Mr Crouch?'

'No, I said it was a scream, my sister thought it was some pigs.'

'At any rate, you both thought it came from a spot where the motor van was passing?'

'Yes.'

'And when you got there, there was nothing to see, and the van had passed?'

'Yes.'

The judge was asked if he wanted to ask the witness any questions. He turned to Mr Crouch. 'The scream sounded as if it came from the road and not from the wood near Farley Hill House?'

'Yes, my Lord,' said Mr Crouch solemnly.

The ever-hopeful Mr Elam made his parting shot. 'Did it sound more like the scream of a child or an animal?'

'A child.'

Tom Sands, a Broadmoor nurse, was called next. He was one of the officers involved in Straffen's recapture and he had sat next to him in the car on the return trip to Broadmoor.

'On the way back I asked him what his intentions were in escaping, and did he mean harm to any of the children he was seen talking to. He replied no, his intentions were to prove his innocence.'

Mr Manningham-Buller waded in to ask, 'Did he also say to you, as you were travelling back in the car, "I have finished with crime"?'

'That is correct.'

'And "As I was with the children I saw you coming after me, so I ran away"?'

'Yes.'

'Had you any idea that any child was missing, or had been killed?'

'No, none at all,' replied Tom Sands and, taking one last look at John Straffen in the dock, he stepped down from the witness box after being thanked for his evidence by the judge.

29

With the facts of the case and what John Straffen might or might not have said out of the way the prosecution case was looking stronger than ever. It was now up to the defence to try to show that their client was insane if they were going to save him from the gallows.

The court guide for insanity comes under the M'Naghten Rules, laid down in 1843 when Daniel McNaughton tried to assassinate the British Prime Minister, Robert Peel, but shot his secretary instead. Under the rules to establish insanity the accused must show he or she was suffering under a defect of reason, from disease of the mind, so as not to know the nature of the act or, if they did know it, that they did not know they were doing wrong.

There are several difficulties facing a defendant considering using this defence. If successful you will be sent to an institution like Broadmoor for an indefinite period until you are deemed sufficiently recovered to be released, if ever. So it's not a defence to be used lightly. You have to show you were suffering from a disease of the mind, that is that you were mentally ill rather than, for instance, losing your temper, however justified losing your temper in the circumstances might be. You then have to show you didn't know what you were doing or, if you did, that you didn't know that what you were doing was legally, rather than morally, wrong.

Everyone in the courtroom at Winchester could see something was wrong with John Straffen. He sat slouched in the dock, his mouth slack, suddenly becoming animated and nodding at the witnesses, or chatting to his guards and laughing at some unseen joke, then lapsing into silence again, head down and staring at the floor in front of his feet. But the question remained as to whether he was mad or just mentally retarded, or was he so retarded to be mad?

As they wouldn't have the opportunity to hear from Straffen directly, the jury would have to rely on witnesses. One person articulate enough and with professional clout was John's long-suffering Bath probation officer, someone who had known Straffen from just after the start of the Second World War in November 1939, when John first came before the courts as a 9-year-old boy.

Sidney Harding went into the witness box to say he'd first supervised John when he was convicted in the juvenile court for stealing a purse.

'Was his conduct good or bad?' asked Mr Elam.

'His conduct was very unsatisfactory,' said Mr Harding, shaking his head.

'Did he commit any offences while he was under your care?'

'There were offences, such as travelling on the railway without a ticket, for which the Great Western Railway would not prosecute, and larceny from his mother of two shillings, but there was no prosecution in that case either. As a result of his breach of probation I arranged for him to be seen by Dr Gordon, a psychiatrist of the Child Guidance Clinic at Bath, and as a result John was certified.'

'Why did you send Straffen to a psychiatrist?' Mr Elam asked.

Mr Harding drew a weary breath. 'After a time I realised that this boy was a problem case. I did everything I possibly could to assist him, and I had to caution him from time to time, but my cautions had very little effect upon him; he was going from bad to worse. I got to the stage where I could not help him or keep him under control; he seemed to have no thought of doing wrong at any time, and from his behaviour under my supervision I do not think he realised really that he was under probation, although I explained to him from time to time.'

Mr Manningham-Buller wanted to clear up what certifying John Straffen meant in this case. 'My learned friend has twice put it to you that he was certified'. 'While you were looking after him, and afterwards, was Straffen ever certified as *insane*?'

'No, he was certified as a mental defective, as a feeble-minded person requiring supervision and control for their own protection.'

'Then there was no question of him being insane at the age of 10?'

'No question at all.'

'I suppose you told him it was wrong and contrary in law for him to go on stealing and committing petty offences?'

'Yes, many times I cautioned him about those things and his association with boys I did not approve of – he appeared to understand but then he disobeyed me.'

'At the same time, as a result of what you told him, did he know it was wrong for him to do those things?'

'I think from the conversations I had with him that he did know that. He must have known himself it was wrong when he did those things.'

'Did you make any enquiries as to his religious education?'

'In most cases I used to try to help these boys, as they were young, to attend a Sunday school in the district where they were living.'

'Do you know whether or not that at the time Straffen had any knowledge of the Ten Commandments?'

'No, I could not say that,' said Mr Harding, looking up at counsel to make sure he'd heard the question correctly.

Mr Elam was determined to have the last say with his witness. 'When you used to caution Straffen for things he did wrong, did he show any sign of remorse?'

'He just acted in a sullen way; he became sullen.'

'Did some of the many boys who disobeyed you act in the same way when you cautioned them?'

'Many boys have disobeyed me during my period of twenty-seven years as probation officer, but the majority of cases did very well.'

'Was Straffen like the majority of cases?'

'No, he was somewhat different. I realised that just after I had him in my charge; I looked upon him as a problem boy, needing strict supervision, and when I found I was not making any strides with him I thought he should go to see a psychiatrist.'

Having not had huge success with the probation officer, Mr Elam moved on to the doctors, of which there was no shortage in this trial. When it comes to insanity in a trial, it is inevitable that the court turns for help to the doctors, although many judges dread doctors giving evidence as each one will give a different diagnosis. However, for once this was not to be the case.

The first medical expert was Dr Alexander Leitch, a consultant psychiatrist who used to work in the prison service at Horfield Prison, Bristol.

He explained that he saw John Straffen in 1947 before he was certified as a feeble-minded defective. Straffen was then sent to Hortham Colony which, Dr Leitch explained, was a mental defectives' colony at Almondsbury in Gloucestershire. 'I noted that, in addition to his defective intelligence, he also showed little or no moral sense, and no regret or remorse at all for his delinquent acts, but rather he appeared to be proud of them, and he took pleasure in talking about them. He seemed to think it was clever to steal and not to be caught; that there was no disadvantage in stealing so long as one was not caught. He told me of a number of stealing episodes of which he appeared to be quite proud.'

There was a tangible frisson in court at this revelation, with members of the public exchanging whispers, the jury glancing at the dock, the judge looking up from his notebook at the witness, and Straffen himself muttering something to his warders and putting his head back down to his chest with a smile.

Mr Elam then turned to a question that had troubled the court throughout the proceedings: what did it really mean to give someone a mental age half his real age?

'The mental age is a figure which is arrived at by means of giving certain tests,' explained Dr Leitch. 'For example, there are a number of questions which every normal child of, say, 8 years of age can answer, but which an average age of 7 cannot answer, and so on through the scale. I found that he could pass those tests which the average nine-and-a-half-year-old child could pass, no more. The average individual has an intelligence level of 100, and this man has 65 per cent of the average.'

'When did you see him next?' asked Mr Elam.

'I next saw him on 29 August 1951 when he was on remand on a capital charge relating to the Bath cases. I also saw him on 1 October 1951, and when he was having an electroencephalograph examination on 7 September. I found his physical condition as a tall, spare but muscular young man, with no evidence of physical disease.'

As afraid of losing the judge as he was of losing the jury, Mr Elam asked, 'Can you explain, in non-technical language, what is an electroencephalograph?'

'The electroencephalograph test is a test which is used to study the functioning of the brain by recording the minute electrical currents which go on in the living brain. These minute electrical currents are picked up by this machine and are amplified many times and are then transferred on to a moving band of paper by means of ink pencils. The result here indicated an abnormal functioning of the brain. The test indicated a severe and widespread disorganisation of those parts of the brain which are thought to control the higher mental processes. This test was repeated one month later, and the results were the same. A second test was made at the Maudsley Hospital in London with similar results.'

'Did you have every source of information for your examinations?' asked Mr Elam.

'I did. I read all the statements and interviewed the accused's mother. I learnt that the grandfather on his mother's side was a patient in Wells Mental Hospital suffering from religious mania. I formed the opinion that his history clearly showed his social incapacity, his inability to cope with ordinary situations, to cope with problems, and to profit by experience. He was unable to foresee the real nature and consequences of his acts. He was unduly impulsive, so that he acted without normal aforethought and without the normal realisation of where his acts were leading him, and of the true consequences of his acts. He showed a complete lack of normal feeling about certain acts; he showed no regret or remorse for acts which normal people would only regard with horror.

'The best example I can give would be the Bath case. He has told me that in this case he had taken a small girl to the cinema, and when leaving the cinema the idea came to him to kill the little girl. When I asked him why, he stated he wanted to annoy the police, because he hated them. He said he hated them because they shadowed him and followed him about, and they had been doing that ever since he was at Hortham Colony, when he left the colony to go home at weekends and in holiday periods, and tried to pin crimes on him that he had not committed. When I asked him if to kill the little girl seemed a sensible thing to do, he replied that it did. When I enquired why, and would it not have been easier to annoy the police by stealing, and he said it was easier to kill the little girl. He said that after this crime he went home and on his way home he bought some fish and chips and ate them on the way home. He then took his usual supper of bread and milk, went to bed and slept soundly, and in the morning he was surprised when the police called at his house; he could not understand why they were there.

'He told me that he knew he was suspected of the first little girl and yet, in spite of knowing he was suspected of that, this second dreadful crime happens – which in my opinion is evidence of his lack of judgment and reasoning.'

Mr Elam felt at last he was getting somewhere. 'Doctor Leitch, you said his IQ was 65 and his mental age that of a nine-and-a half-year-old child, but does the matter stop there?'

'No, I think it goes further. I think his defects were deeper than mere lack of intelligence, that the majority of children at nine-and-a-half would show more ability to learn by experience and to foresee the results of their acts, and would show more appreciation of right and wrong than he did. I also consider that the nature of his impulses was abnormal. I will give two examples. He was angry with a girl he knew, and he expressed his anger by wringing the necks of a number of chickens belonging to her father; and he was angry with the police, and he expressed his anger by killing someone.'

'We are all familiar with children breaking their toys,' said Mr Elam. 'Does that have anything to do with it?'

'The normal young child may express its anger in explosive outbursts by perhaps destroying its toys, or breaking something; that is the conduct one expects from a normal small child. This young man of 21 or 22 now shows the same impulsive outbursts in response to situations that make him angry. What would be relatively normal for a young child, of course, is grossly abnormal in a man of 22.

'The other aspect of it is equally important in that he does not show the normal emotional responses to conduct. No normal person would contemplate doing such acts without feeling reluctant, or having feelings of revulsion, but in this case there was an almost complete absence of feeling. He told me that he was not disturbed at all while he was doing these things. He appears to have had no more feeling in doing them than a normal person would have in killing a fly. Those were the views he expressed consistently at the time. His appreciation of his present position shows the same inability to judge his circumstances. He has told me on three separate occasions when I have seen him in connection with this case of Linda Bowyer that he is quite happy, and that he is not worrying about anything, and that he does not mind being hanged.'

Mr Elam looked at his watch and found he was running out of time before the court adjourned at the end of the second day. 'Can you express any opinion about the killings, or about sadism, Dr Leitch?' he asked.

'As far as I know, and from my discussions with him, it seems to me in the case of Cicely Batstone, to which he confessed freely and which he is quite prepared to talk about freely, he was unable to visualise the horror and the pain the little girl must have suffered, and quite unable to realise the grief and pain her parents must have suffered. In other words, the act did not have meaning for him, and the true consequences, which such an act would have for a normal individual.'

Dr Leitch was saying that John Straffen showed neither empathy for his victims in how they must have suffered in the way they met their deaths, nor any regret for what he did to them to get back at the police for annoying him.

30

By the start of the third day of a trial, things are beginning to relax a little. Court ushers are busying around trying to put in urgent cases like injunctions before the main trial resumes, while counsel and solicitors are now on first-name terms and sharing each others' peppermints. Then there's the judge himself, treated with obsequious courtesy whatever his foibles, whether it's the time he needs to write down the evidence in laborious longhand, deafness or the ability to look asleep when he's bored.

So with the stage set for the third day, with proceedings running to full reviews in the national newspapers and the jurors behaving themselves in their local pubs and clubs, Mr Justice Cassels entered court and as usual was shown to his chair by his clerk, leaning over the bench to open his red notebook and carefully unscrew the cap of his fountain pen.

There was a moment's silence while the judge found his place in the notebook, and nodded towards counsel. Mr Elam asked if he might continue with Dr Leitch's evidence, and on receiving a further nod asked the good doctor to resume his place in the witness box.

'Dr Leitch, you have seen John Straffen several times recently,' said Mr Elam. 'Can you describe his mental condition for us, please?'

Not to be outdone by the judge, Dr Leitch opened his own notebook. 'His mental condition showed only slight changes from when I saw him last year. He has become more familiar, in a glib way, with the procedure in court, and the use of terms which one hears in court – such as guilty and not guilty, and things like that; but his intelligence is no higher, and I don't think he shows any better reasoning capacity, any better ability to foresee the future and to plan, and generally to deal with situations as a normal person would. As a result I am satisfied he is now certifiable as a feeble-minded mental defective suffering from a defect of reason, and I define "reason" here as the ability to think logically and clearly.'

Mr Elam edged his way through the M'Naghten Rules on the question of defining insanity. 'Is this kind of mental defectiveness from which Straffen is suffering in your view "a disease of the mind"?' he asked.

'In my opinion, it can rightly be included within the broad term "disease of the mind". It may be that from the strictly medical point of view that might be regarded as controversial, but I know of no legal definition of "disease of the mind", and the use of these terms legally and medically differs very considerably. I should say he only knew the nature and quality of the act he was doing in a modified way, within the limits of his low intelligence as a mental defective. The conclusion I drew from a series of questions I put to him was that he was unable to separate "wrong" in the ethical sense from "illegal". This is another example of his defect of reason, due to his mental defectiveness, although superficially he appears to be normal.'

When it came to Mr Manningham-Buller's turn to cross-examine Dr Leitch, he didn't take long to show his contempt for doctors generally, and for Dr Leitch in particular. 'Would you say that murderers that have come under your care showed a due regard for their victims that an average individual would show?' he asked, without looking at Dr Leitch but into a far corner of the court instead.

'I cannot speak for the actual moment of the murder, but immediately afterwards, yes.'

'It may be because of the consequences to themselves immediately afterwards; but I am talking about the moment of the murder – from the moment they intended or decided to commit the murder, to the execution of the act?'

'I cannot claim to have any exact knowledge of what is in the mind of a murderer at the time he commits the crime,' said Dr Leitch quietly.

'I am not asking that,' replied counsel tartly. 'I am asking you this question: would you not agree that the majority of murderers do not show the regard that an average human being would have for the feelings of others?'

'Speaking of the actual moment of the murder, I should say that it is true; but it is not true of the time preceding and following it.'

Mr Manningham-Buller looked at the witness for the first time. 'If you will just answer the question we shall save a great deal of time,' he growled like an irate schoolmaster. 'Do you think it is not true of the average murderer that, before committing the murder, he has not the same regard for the consequences of his act as a normal average person would have?'

'I should say only just before,' said Dr Leitch cautiously, 'only in the time immediately preceding the act.'

'Then let's turn to the question of feeble-mindedness within the definition of the Mental Deficiency Act, that is to say a person "in whose case there exists mental defectiveness which, though not amounting to imbecility, is yet so pronounced that they require care, supervision and control". If that is the definition which correctly fits Straffen's case, then in your view is he insane?'

'From the medical point of view, he is not insane,' replied Dr Leitch.

The Solicitor General let this reply register before he went on to ask some more questions about what Straffen thought he was doing at the time of the killings, and then let Dr Leitch go as suddenly as a dog dropping a ball in a game of fetch.

Mr Park, junior counsel for the defence, then called his namesake Dr Peter Parkes, who'd worked under Dr Leitch at Bristol, and who had given evidence at Taunton Assizes resulting in John Straffen being found unfit to plead and sent to Broadmoor.

As he gave his evidence it became clear that Dr Parkes had shifted his position about his former patient's fitness to plead from last time, for no more complicated reason than Straffen's exposure to various doctors since then, and talking endlessly about his case to fellow patients at Broadmoor.

'This experience made him much more familiar with words like guilty, jury, right and wrong, and the answers he gave me on subsequent visits were very, very different to the ones he gave to me when he was at Bristol. He seems to have a much better knowledge of court procedure, and seems to know the answers to many of the usual questions which medical witnesses are likely to ask prisoners in this type of case,' said Dr Parkes.

This was all red rag to a bull for Mr Manningham-Buller, who was already scraping one hoof on the ground before he stood to cross-examine the doctor. 'Assume for a moment, Dr Parkes, that Straffen killed Linda Bowyer. Have you any reason to suppose that he did not know what he was doing when he put his hand on her throat and any reason to suppose he did not do it with the intention of killing her?'

'No,' replied the beleaguered Dr Parkes.

'You gave evidence at the Taunton Assizes that Straffen was unfit to plead. Do you still hold that view now?'

There was hardly a pause before the answer. 'No, I hold the view now that he is fit to plead.'

Junior counsel stood up again like a boxer who, already losing on points, had just been delivered the knock-out blow. 'You said something about his moral sense?' he asked, clutching at straws.

'I should say he has very little moral sense. We heard evidence that when he was interviewed in Bath he did not realise the seriousness of his position and he laughed. I should have thought that showed a lack of moral sense.'

The judge interrupted here to say the court was not concerned about moral sense: there were many kinds of laughter, hysterical, uncontrolled or stupid. 'But surely a normal man would not laugh in a serious situation – this should be taken into account, in my view, and his general demeanour at the time?' asked Dr Parkes, getting in the last word himself.

The last doctor to be called by the defence was Dr Richard Williams, a medical officer at Broadmoor, but it was the question of John Straffen playing bridge that took up most of the discussion. The Solicitor General, who looked like a man who might have played bridge in his Oxford days, asked Dr Williams if Straffen had learnt to play contract bridge in his time at Broadmoor.

'I could not say, because I have no knowledge of contract bridge; so I cannot say how successful he was,' replied Dr Williams.

'I did not ask you how successful he was,' snapped Mr Manningham-Buller. 'I asked you whether he has learnt to play contract bridge since he has been in Broadmoor?'

'I can only say he has attempted it, but I could not say with what degree of success,' replied Dr Williams cautiously, stepping back in the witness box.

'Did you ask him any questions about his knowledge of the Ten Commandments?' asked counsel.

'No,' replied Dr Williams bluntly.

After Mr Manningham-Buller had dealt with him, junior counsel for the defence popped up again. 'Did you have a record sheet relating to Straffen when he was in Broadmoor; if so, is there any reference there to the fact that he is trying to learn contract bridge, or words to that effect?'

'Yes, there is reference to the fact that he is trying to learn. It is in my handwriting, but it is recorded in a rather jocular sense.'

The question of exactly what had been written was not pursued, and a relieved Mr Elam got to his feet to tell the judge that that concluded the case for the defence.

Mr Manningham-Buller got up to say he now wanted to call a doctor or two to respond to the evidence of the defence doctors.

Dr John Mathieson was first up. He was Principal Medical Officer at Brixton Prison and he had seen Straffen nearly every day for a month while he was in Brixton before going to Wandsworth. Dr Mathieson told of how Straffen had given a very clear account of his activities for the period after he escaped from Broadmoor.

'It was clear and coherent,' Dr Mathieson said. 'He needed very little prompting. He did at one time go over some plans and photographs, and he was able to identify the places on the plans from the photographs; and indeed when I made a wrong interpretation on one occasion, he corrected me.'

'Did you speak to him about his knowledge of right and wrong?' asked the Solicitor General.

'At first he told me he took his standards of right and wrong from his mother's teaching, and he expressed a good deal of affection for this mother. Later he told me, as regards whether killing was right or wrong, that in the Bible there was a commandment, and he quoted the words "Thou shalt not kill". He said that if you killed a person you could be punished, and should be punished.'

'While he was in Brixton, did he read a good deal?' asked the Solicitor General, at last getting somewhere with the Ten Commandments.

'He read quite a lot. He would pick up a paper, such as *Picture Post*, and start to read, and very quickly – and this is reported to me by the officers under whose care he was – then get tired of reading and go at once to the pictures in the paper.'

'Did you learn that he had been learning or trying to learn the game of contract bridge?'

'I was informed that that was so.'

The Solicitor General couldn't stop now. 'Do *you* play contract bridge?' he asked.

'I have played occasionally,' the doctor replied cautiously.

'Do you have some knowledge of the game?' counsel persisted, with a hint of irritation at everyone being so coy about the game.

'Yes.'

'Did you ask him any questions about the game?'

'No,' replied Dr Mathieson, bringing the game to an end.

When it came to Mr Elam's cross-examination, he wanted to talk more about the electroencephalograph test and, despite the test and Straffen being certified as a mental defective, was it the doctor's opinion that he was not suffering from a disease of the mind?

'Yes, in my opinion it is amentia and not dementia, that is to say a lack of mind, rather than a mind that was there and which has become diseased or demented. In Straffen's case I think it is fair to say there is a history that his mind, or his brain, might have been damaged when he was in India through encephalitis, which may have destroyed certain of the brain cells, which have never been replaced.'

Dr Mathieson was then himself replaced by Dr James Murdoch, Principal Medical Officer at Wandsworth, who'd seen Straffen daily since his transfer from Brixton about three weeks before. The Solicitor General cut immediately to his favourite subject. 'Did you have any conversation with Straffen about his learning to play contract bridge?'

'Yes, this was part of a general conversation about how he employed his spare time and amused himself at Broadmoor. I was a medical officer there myself at one time; I was aware of the conditions there and I wanted to see what knowledge he had of the institution and its surroundings. In the course of the conversation he said that he played bridge there. I said "What kind of bridge?" and he said "Contract; I know there is another kind, but I don't know the name of it".'

The Solicitor General looked almost happy for the first time in the trial. 'Did you ask him any questions to find out to what extent he was able to understand the game?'

'Frankly, I did not think he would know it, so I asked him how many cards there were in the pack, and he correctly answered that question. I asked him the number of suits, and he was correct in that, and he named them. I asked him the number of cards in a hand, and he gave me the correct answer. I then asked him if he knew what a bid meant, and he answered that correctly. Then I said, "Now if I were to make a bid of four hearts, what would that mean?" and he said, "If nobody outbid me, I would play the hand". I said, "How many tricks would you have to take?" and he said, "Ten".'

'And that is the correct number?' asked counsel triumphantly.

'Yes. I did not take him any further on that matter. This is the conversation as I remember it.'

154

'Has he shown any sign of insanity while at Wandsworth?'

'None.'

'He talked to you about his past, did he?'

'Yes, I was more interested in his immediate past. I took him over events from the time before he escaped, and the manner in which he escaped, and he was able to describe it very accurately. Indeed, I had forgotten one little part of the structure of the building, which he was able to recall.'

'Did he tell you anything further about his escape?'

'He informed me that he'd planned his escape ever since he went to Broadmoor. Then he described the manner of his escape and where he went, and he described the whole thing. At one point I asked him how long he had taken to get to a particular place, which was beyond the railway – he having got over the golf course – and I said, "How long were you at liberty?" and he said, "Four or five hours". I said "Why did you take such a long time to get to that spot, because I could walk it in three-quarters of an hour?" and he said, "Yes, but you would know where you were going, and I did not; I had to find my way, and also to dodge the staff who were looking for me". Then he described quite accurately the circumstances of his period of liberty, as is described in his own statement.'

'Is he in your opinion a feeble-minded person?'

'Well, I would place him in a higher category than feeble minded. I made his mental age to be about 12.'

'In your opinion is he sane or insane?'

'In my opinion, he is sane.'

Mr Elam in his cross-examination made the point that by now was in the front of everyone's mind. 'In your opinion he is sane, as an escapee from Broadmoor Institution – do we get to that position?'

'I said he was sane,' repeated the doctor testily.

'Although he had been certified in Broadmoor Institution?'

'Yes.'

'Which is an institution for the insane?'

'Yes, but there are a lot of sane people in Broadmoor,' replied the doctor, which produced a ripple of laughter around the court.

The judge still smiling asked, 'You mean among the patients there?'

'Yes, my lord.'

Mr Elam wasn't convinced. 'Are they kept inside that lunatic asylum although they are sane?'

'There is quite a large number who have recovered their sanity,' replied

Dr Murdoch, although he didn't explain whether it was usual for a patient to recover his sanity after only six months.

'What happens then?' asked Mr Elam.

'They are eventually released.'

Mr Elam didn't let point go. 'If they are alleged to have committed a criminal offence, they can then be tried for that offence if they become sane?'

'Yes, it is possible.'

'Did Straffen come within that category?'

'I wouldn't know. These decisions are made at a very high level.'

The last medical witness to be called by the prosecution was Dr Thomas Munro, a consultant psychologist who had seen John Straffen on four occasions. He said in his opinion, while he came within the feeble-minded group, Straffen was of relatively high intelligence in that group and knew the nature of his act when he killed Linda Bowyer. He wanted to stand trial 'to try to prove myself I did not do this murder'. He knew the punishment for murder was hanging, and he knew the role of a judge and jury in a trial.

Dr Munro reported that Straffen had said it was wrong to murder because it was against the law and one of the commandments.

'Did you ask him what commandment?' asked counsel.

'Yes, he said there are ten of them, are there not? He said they came from God and were in the Bible. He didn't know all of them, but knew most, such as you should not worship idols, you should not steal, and you should not covet thy neighbour's goods. Finally he said you shall not kill.'

Under cross-examination Dr Munro went on to say that his mental condition was probably acquired as a result of the infection of the brain when he was about 3, looking at the medical evidence. This could produce lack of control, and even violent behaviour. The lack of an obvious reason for such action, he explained, is one of the clinical characteristics of behaviour due to brain damage.

As a weary Mr Elam sat down, Mr Manningham-Buller rose to say he was calling no further medical evidence.

31

So Mr Elam had to get back on his feet to deliver the closing speech for the defence. He probably knew it was a lost cause from the moment the judge allowed the evidence of the Bath murders to be included, and any hope of his client being returned to Broadmoor was lost after failing to find a doctor – not even Dr Parkes – who was willing to say John Straffen was insane.

Mr Elam emphasised that what few local witnesses he had been able to produce were obviously 'as honest as the day was long' in dealing with the scream they'd heard that evening, and repeated that Mr Crouch was an ex-royal servant with the implication that his evidence should carry that bit more weight. The prosecution was saying that the scream was later than when Linda Bowyer died, and Dr Teare might have said that Linda wouldn't have screamed once the hands were on her throat, but what might have happened before that, when she saw something in the murderer's eyes, or saw his hands coming towards her?

Mr Elam added that the case would not be decided on whether John Straffen played bridge, or that he laughed when being questioned by the police when he apparently failed to see what a serious position he was in. He briefly referred to the medical evidence where it was unusual for so many doctors to be in agreement on both sides. The only difference was that the prosecution were saying that Straffen knew perfectly well what he was doing, while the defence said he knew what he was doing, but only within the confines of his limited intelligence.

The Solicitor General in his closing speech said that the defence was relying on two arguments: firstly that Straffen had not been proved to have killed Linda Bowyer, and second that if he did kill her, then anyway he was insane and not responsible in law for killing her.

No one was disputing he was feeble minded, he added, with the intelligence of a child of nine and a half or a little more, and that he was at the top of the feeble-minded category – but not one of the doctors thought Straffen insane. Much had been made of Straffen knowing what he was doing within the limits of his intelligence, but the extent to which we know anything is limited by our intelligence. If it was beyond the realms of his intelligence, then he could not have known it; but they all agreed that he knew the nature and quality of his act, and that he knew it was legally, rather than morally or ethically, wrong.

On the question of whether Straffen actually murdered Linda Bowyer, the jury had heard details of the Bath murders and the similarities between those two murders and the murder of Linda Bowyer. He also referred to the similarity in Straffen going off to have fish and chips after murdering Cicely Batstone, and in Linda Bowyer's case calmly having tea and biscuits at Farley Hill House.

Finally the Solicitor General dealt with Straffen's response to the police when being asked in Broadmoor next morning whether he got up to 'any mischief' while on the run for those four hours and immediately saying he did not kill the little girl – and later that he did not kill the little girl with the bicycle – when no one had suggested anyone had been attacked or killed.

Mr Manningham-Buller sat down on his seat with a clatter and threw his notes on the desk in front of him with the air of someone who'd had his time wasted by a defence daring to suggest their client might not be guilty of the charge.

While the judge had sat there presiding over the trial for the last three days, making copious notes and intervening occasionally to ask a question or two of a witness, the time now came for his main performance in the proceedings. The charge to the jury, or summing up speech, had to be a finely balanced exercise weighing up the evidence for both sides, without seeming to be prejudicial in any way, sprinkling the speech with warnings to the jury to be as impartial as possible, and saying whether certain parts of the evidence should be given more or less weight.

Every judge was also aware that his words would be carefully studied afterwards to see if there was any scope for an appeal.

Mr Justice Cassels created a scrupulously fair, almost avuncular image, and this image was only strengthened when he started his address with what sounded like a bedtime story.

'Members of the jury, about a mile from the boundary line which runs between this county and the County of Berkshire, and in the County of Berkshire there lies the little village of Farley Hill. It is a very small village; it consists of a few bungalows and cottages, a shop, a school and a church, and through it there runs a road – a road you may well think not very frequented – and in that village there live a number of people who, doubtless, have carried on their work there and lived quiet and useful lives with their children.'

A picture was being drawn of a corner of rustic England where there was always honey for tea, where old ladies would always have someone to see them over the road, and where it would be no surprise to see Noddy and Big Ears drive up the high street in pursuit of a masked burglar with a bag of swag slung over his back.

'Upon 29 April an excitement must have come to that village of Farley Hill,' continued Mr Justice Cassels, 'when it was known that a little girl, by name Linda Bowyer, five-and-a-half years of age, known to everybody in the village, whose mother lived at Pillar Box Cottage, was missing.'

The jury was now in the judge's thrall – even Mr Manningham-Buller was listening, face turned up to the bench, giving his lordship the rapt attention he once gave to his nanny in the nursery.

'She had been seen during the afternoon of that day riding her bicycle with her little friends along that road – in both directions, I think. Then, a little later, the children with whom she had been seen playing were there, but she was not, and her mother, as is only natural, began to worry after a little time. Then her failure to come home led to her stepfather communicating with the police. That night of anxiety, not only to the mother and stepfather, but to everybody else in that village, came to an end when, at twenty-five minutes past five the next morning Inspector Brazell discovered her little bicycle about twenty-eight yards away from the boundary of the road, in a copse in a field. A quarter of an hour later, and further into the field and not far from the edge of a wood or copse, her body was found. She was dead. She may well have lain there all night.'

This was no longer a fairy story. The images brought home to the jury the enormity of what had happened; for the parents it was another bleak reminder of their loss.

John Straffen's eyes remained fixed on the judge, hanging on his every word, wondering what was going to happen next.

The judge went through the number of sightings of Linda and Straffen in the high street and their various timings. He described the chronology of the escape from Broadmoor, exactly where it happened and how it happened.

'You might think a notice could almost have been put up in the institution at such a place as this lean-to shed – a notice indicating that this was the Way Out,' he added without a smile.

He went through the visits to Mrs Spencer, Mrs Sims's caravan, and to the nanny and Mrs Kenyon at Farley Hill House, and then the lift from Mrs Miles. He passed on to John's response to the police once back in Broadmoor and the full written statement made to them; the Bath murders and the issue of insanity. Here he reminded the jury that if any patient escapes from Broadmoor it doesn't mean that they commit murder with impunity; the question remains, was he insane at the time he committed the act?

Whether or not Mr Justice Cassels was a bridge player we don't know, but he wanted to deal with the issue. 'I would venture to suggest to you that you may well think that that does not carry you very much further. It may well perhaps lead you to suppose that although suffering from a certain amount of mental defectiveness, none the less he is able to understand cards, and to use them in such a game. It may perhaps be within your knowledge that some people who do not present a very strong mental picture to the world are able to do elaborate calculations.'

After going through the medical evidence, and the prisoner's previous convictions and probation problems, the judge came to his conclusions.

'It is a great responsibility which you bear as a jury of citizens. You try one of the most serious charges that can be brought against anybody in this country. You may have had many feelings as you have listened to this case. As those three mothers came into that witness box to tell you about the little girls they have lost, a feeling of sympathy must have risen in your minds, but dismiss it. You are not to give a verdict against this man because you sympathise with those three unfortunate mothers.'

Finally he turned to the role of Broadmoor in all this.

'As you have listened to this case you may well have reflected that it was a great pity that he ever escaped from Broadmoor. You have not been called into that jury box in order to discover who may be blamed for that escape. That has nothing to do with this court. You are not trying the Broadmoor Institution: you are trying John Thomas Straffen for the crime of murder. It is a serious thing, is murder; no more serious charge can be made. So also is the death of a human being a serious thing. No verdict that you may give will bring that little girl back to life, but the state comes forward and alleges, and seeks to prove, that murder has been committed by a grown human being upon a little and defenceless girl.'

It was 1.20 p.m. on the fourth day of the trial and the judge had been speaking for four hours, when he asked the jury to retire and consider their verdict.

32

lready concerned that he had overrun the usual lunch hour by twenty minutes, Mr Justice Cassels wasted no time in shedding his robes in his chambers behind the courtroom. He walked out to his car to be driven back to his lodgings at the eighteenth-century town house near the cathedral, hoping that he was not putting the staff there to inconvenience.

As he sat back in the leathered opulence of the official car, the judge sighed with relief at completing the case, despite the false start – he hadn't decided what to do with the errant juror who presumably was still in the court buildings somewhere. As to Straffen, it was never pleasant to condemn a prisoner to death, but in a case of murder he had no choice if it came to it and justice had to take its course. There had been some interesting legal submissions on the decision to allow the inclusion of the Bath murders, and he'd kept control of Manningham-Buller and stopped him browbeating the defence witnesses too much. The doctors had not been too tedious and seemed for once to be agreeing rather than fighting. Broadmoor could be sorted out later with an enquiry about security, and he hadn't had to criticise the Reading Magistrates for not returning Straffen to Broadmoor when it was pretty obvious that it would have been risky, if not provocative to the public, to do so.

Mr Justice Cassels thought how he might spend the afternoon, catching up with some paperwork, preparing for another trial in the following week, and then getting an early train back up to London to join his wife for the weekend. The jury had four days' worth of evidence to sift through, and would need some time to discuss the issue of insanity at least. He'd be surprised if they reached a verdict by close of play that day, and thought probably Monday would be the earliest he saw them again. If he'd put money on the date and time of the verdict, then he would go for some time Monday afternoon.

So it came as something of a surprise when, after tackling the lukewarm tomato soup, his clerk walked in to say the jury was ready with a verdict after only half an hour. They'd hardly had time to eat their sandwiches, let alone go through the medical evidence if they were so sure of facts.

Feeling like Drake finishing his game of bowls, the judge said he would at least finish his soup before coming back to court. Anyway, if it came to it, it wasn't a good idea to sentence a man to death on an empty stomach.

Back at court the police were ready to escort the judge back into the building, where he put on his robes, still almost warm from when he had shed them before lunch. He followed his clerk into the courtroom. The jury was already in their box, looking calm but resigned, and as John Straffen was for the last time brought up into the dock, still talking to his warders, it became obvious that the twelve members of the jury were looking anywhere but at the prisoner, always a bad sign for the defence when it came to the verdict.

The clerk to the court told the prisoner to stay standing and turned to the foreman of the jury.

'Members of the jury, are you all agreed upon your verdict?' he asked.

'We are,' said the foreman, and cleared his throat.

'Do you find the prisoner at the bar, John Thomas Straffen, guilty or not guilty upon this indictment?'

'Guilty.'

'And that is the verdict of you all?'

'It is.'

There was a murmur of approval from the public gallery, every member of which turned to look at John Straffen, who remained staring vacantly at the judge without a glance at the jury.

The clerk jotted the verdict on a piece of paper in front of him, and turned his attention to the prisoner.

'John Thomas Straffen, you stand convicted of murder. Have you anything to say why the court should not give you judgment of death, according to law?' he asked.

John stood motionless in the dock, gawping at the clerk and trying to absorb what was being said to him.

The judge's clerk, who'd had a moment of panic earlier trying to find the black cloth that was used on these occasions, solemnly and rather untidily placed the cloth over the judge's wig. The clerk then stepped back with the relief of a best man who'd discharged his duty by handing the ring to the groom. He checked that the prison chaplain drafted from Wandsworth Prison was standing next to him to listen to the sentence.

Mr Justice Cassels' tummy was rumbling.

'John Thomas Straffen, the jury have found you guilty, and rightly found you guilty, of the crime of wilful murder,' he started. 'It was a cruel and brutal act you committed, knowingly, upon that day. For that crime the law provides but one penalty. The sentence of the court is that you be taken from this place to a lawful prison, and thence to a place of execution, and there suffer death by hanging, and that your body be buried within the precincts of the prison in which you shall have been last confined before your execution, and may the Lord have mercy upon your soul.'

'Amen,' intoned the chaplain.

There was a short silence where nobody seemed to know what to do next, the sort of silence you get at the end of a church service after the blessing where it seems indecent to leave too quickly. Mrs Straffen in the public gallery sobbed quietly. The judge nodded at the four warders, two of whom gripped the prisoner by an arm to lead him down to the cells.

After dispatching the prisoner Mr Justice Cassels now directed his attentions to the juror who had caused the false start at the beginning of the trial. Mr William Gladwin was brought before the court, along with a barrister who'd been hired to speak on his behalf. There was some difficulty in knowing where to put Mr Gladwin: the dock didn't seem appropriate, although his demeanour suggested he was well and truly in the dock, nor was a seat next to his barrister the place. So he stood awkwardly in front of the barristers' bench, his hands joined in front of him, shifting nervously from foot to foot.

William Gladwin was a well-built man in his early thirties, with a shock of black hair above a short back and sides, who looked like he'd done his bit serving his country in the war and was now facing Mr Cassels in the same way he might have faced his commanding officer on a charge.

Mr Norman Broderick stood to represent his client and started by saying that the details of this incident as reported didn't quite match what actually happened on this unfortunate occasion. He also said that there was nothing deliberate and malicious about Mr Gladwin's behaviour and that it was only as the result of a remark made to him by someone that he said what he did.

'In my experience,' said counsel, 'I have never come across someone who is so anxious he has done wrong, and so contrite of all the trouble and expense he had caused.'

The judge pondered these remarks a moment, and then turned to the hapless Mr Gladwin.

'Mr Gladwin, I hope you will never have the experience of having to sit in the dock. If you did I wonder what your state of mind would be as you sat there, after seeing a jury sworn in to give a verdict according to the evidence, and then for you to hear that the moment they left the box they were going to talk to other people about the case, and were going to give a verdict according to what other people had told them, and not on the evidence?

'It was wrong, a wicked discharge of your duties as a citizen, to have allowed yourself to express an opinion about a case which you were trying as a juryman, especially after I had given my warning that you were not to say anything or discuss the case.'

Mr Gladwin looked more and more despondent as this homily went on, convinced now he was going to be given a spell in prison to see what that was like first-hand.

'I daresay you are wondering what is going to happen to you,' continued the judge. 'I will relieve you of that anxiety. I shall not fine you, but I do want the importance of what you have done and your experience to be known far and wide.'

He then raised a finger at the beleaguered juror.

'You have put the expenses of this trial up by a great sum of money and I suppose worst of all was that you caused the unfortunate mother of that little girl to come back again and tell her sorry story, and just because you could not keep your tongue quiet.'

With that a magnanimous Mr Justice Cassels got to his feet, picked up his notebook and left the court. It was only just gone two-thirty on Friday afternoon and he was going to catch the early London train after all.

33

Mr Elam, his junior barrister and solicitor made their way down from the courtroom to the cells to see their client. The immediate aftermath of a guilty verdict is never an easy time for a defence team and its client; it is rather more difficult when the client has just been condemned to death.

The three lawyers were shown into an interview room by a prison officer. They were not saying a lot, giving Mr Elam time to compose what he was going to say to his client.

In what seemed seconds only John Straffen was shown in and given the fourth seat at the table. The expression on his face was more like that of a man receiving the news of a modest win on the pools than someone under a death sentence. He grinned at his legal team and nodded, his mouth working but not saying anything.

'I'm sorry we couldn't get you a better result, Mr Straffen', Mr Elam said kindly.

John lowered his head then looked up at him. 'They're hanging me because I did the two murders but not the third one,' he said.

Mr Elam didn't hurry his reply. 'They found you guilty of the third murder, Linda Bowyer. You were only being tried for the third one.'

John thought about this and nodded again. 'Are we going to appeal? I might get off,' he asked.

'I wanted to talk to you about that. There are two possible grounds of appeal.'

John smiled a big, goofy smile. 'I didn't do it. That's one of them.'

'That probably wouldn't be the best approach in this case. That's not what I had in mind. It would be on the grounds that the judge shouldn't have allowed evidence of the Bath murders to be considered in this trial; and that you should have been cautioned by the police officers when they came to see you in Broadmoor on the morning after your escape.'

John thought about this. 'They shouldn't have mentioned the Bath murders. I confessed to those.'

'That's not why the judge allowed it.'

'They didn't have any witnesses to those. That was why they sent me to Broadmoor, I reckon.'

Mr Elam shook his head. 'Well, we'll appeal on the Bath point.'

John laughed and thumped the table. 'There you are – I'm doing all the work for you,' he said.

'And the point about the lack of a caution in Broadmoor.'

'That's right,' John repeated. 'That's the second time they've questioned me first thing in the morning. I was sleepy. They should have cautioned me they were coming.'

Mr Elam made a short note. 'Right then, I'll get grounds of appeal drafted up and your solicitor will show it to you. Is there anything you want – they'll be taking you back to Wandsworth shortly, I imagine. Would you like to see the chaplain?'

John considered this. 'Would that go well for me, showing that I was religious?'

'That's a matter for you, Mr Straffen.'

'I'd rather see my mum.'

'That may not be possible here – more likely back at Wandsworth,' replied Mr Elam, and stood to solemnly shake hands with his client.

'Does it hurt?' asked John, as he grasped Mr Elam's hand.

'Does what hurt?'

'Getting hanged – does it hurt, d'you think?'

'That's a question I can't answer. I'm sorry. Why not wait until after the appeal, eh?'

'Oh, there is one thing you could do for me, Mr Elam,' said John as he was escorted to the door by an officer.

'Of course, what's that?'

'Give me a lift to the station,' said John, and he slapped his sides at the joke he'd made a hundred times to lawyers over the years.

When he reached Wandsworth Prison John found he was no longer in his cell but placed in the execution suite as a condemned prisoner. Here he was given a larger and more comfortable room with two windows. On the other side of the room, unknown to the prisoner, was a wardrobe hiding a door leading straight to the scaffold, where at eight o'clock on the appointed morning he would be met on the far side of the door by the prison governor, a chaplain, and the hangman, Mr Pierrepoint.

Mr Pierrepoint reckoned on spending not longer than thirty seconds to a minute on getting the prisoner from his room to the drop.

As John made himself comfortable on the bunk he reflected on how important he'd become in the last few months, meriting the mayor and alderman at the first Bath hearing, then a couple of judges at his trials, a chaplain and now a special suite in prison. He'd have his meals brought to him here, and special prison guards to sit with him day and night on suicide watch in case he harmed himself. A black flag would be run up on the mast over the prison on the day and an announcement posted on the prison doors to confirm to the world the execution had been carried out.

But he was sure the appeal would succeed. He still couldn't see how they could convict him for anything without witnesses. No one had actually seen him kill those girls. The only reason he'd been convicted of the Bath murders was because he'd confessed. He hadn't confessed to the one after the escape and that's why the appeal court would set him free.

Whatever they did they wouldn't be sending him back to Broadmoor. He couldn't face that, being told to do cleaning duties around the buildings and jobs in the garden. He'd told them all in Broadmoor that if you escaped they didn't send you back. At least in prison they didn't make you do jobs. He'd finished with crime; he'd told the staff that in the car coming back to Broadmoor. If they put him back in prison he wouldn't mind. He didn't want to annoy the police or the prison staff any more – he'd make their tea if they wanted, as long as they didn't tell him to do it. If they did, he'd escape again – he knew he could now.

His only regret about the escape from Broadmoor at the time had been not bringing Rupert. But he'd got him back now with the rest of his belongings and he propped the bear up beside him on the bunk. If they hanged him he'd ask that Rupert be buried with him. They'd do that for him – that'd be his last wish and they always granted you your last wish.

The execution was set for Thursday 4 September 1952.

34

The Court of Criminal Appeal is situated in the labyrinth of courts making up the Royal Courts of Justice on the Strand, London. Entering the building from the Strand into a hall with the dimensions and gothic splendour of a cathedral is an intimidating experience for the first-time visitor, and brings home the maxim laid down by Lord Coke in the seventeenth century: 'Be you ever so high, the law is above you'.

On 20 August 1952 the same legal teams that had appeared at the Winchester Assize filed into the Royal Courts of Justice and made their way up twisting flights of stone stairs and corridors to a courtroom that hadn't changed since the day it was built in the second half of the nineteenth century. The judges' bench was raised higher than in the Winchester courtroom and seemed almost to touch the ceiling, with a long drop to the clerks' desk in front of the bench – about the length of the drop from the scaffold in Her Majesty's prisons – where the clerks chattered among themselves with little or no attention to what was going on in the judicial heights above them. Ushers bustled in and out of court with pieces of paper in their hand like furtive lovers delivering *billets-doux*.

When John was brought up into the dock to await the arrival of the judges, no one even bothered to look up. One or two members of the press sat back in their box twiddling their pencils, and what few members of the public had navigated their way through the corridors coughed and shuffled their feet in the public seats at the back of the court, waiting for something to happen.

Mr Elam felt he should say something to his client, even if to steady his nerves and to try to make him feel at home. But he needn't have bothered. John, dressed today in a voluminous prison suit, was engrossed in conversation with his warders, and his counsel decided if he was happy then let him be.

Only when he'd turned back from the dock did Mr Elam notice Mrs Straffen enter the public gallery and give him a shy smile.

As ten o'clock approached an air of expectancy filled the court, like a theatre audience aware that the stage curtain was about to go up. Then suddenly the court was on its feet, watching three judges enter from stage right, wearing black, silk gowns and short wigs. Mr Justice Slade, Mr Justice Devlin, and Mr Justice Gorman took their seats, with Mr Justice Slade sitting in the centre between his colleagues as the one that morning who would give judgment on behalf of the three of them, if all three agreed.

Mr Elam was asked to address the court on the issues and once again went through the question of whether the trial judge should have allowed evidence of the Bath murders in trying the third murder, and then whether the police officers should have cautioned John Straffen at Broadmoor before questioning him on what he got up to while free.

Then Mr Justice Slade, after telling the Solicitor General they didn't need to hear from him, launched into his judgment, taking the cautioning question first. In this case, he said, the trial judge took the view that 'in custody' meant in the custody of the police and didn't apply to a patient in Broadmoor. The court agreed with this view and considered there was no substance in that ground of appeal at all.

Mr Justice Slade said the other ground of appeal raised a far more serious point. He said the general rule, of course, was that evidence that the accused had been guilty of criminal acts other than the one covered by the indictment should be excluded. But certain similar fact evidence was admissible, not to show the accused person had a criminal character, but that he might have committed the specific offence with which he was charged. This might be a pattern of events that went beyond coincidence, or a system to show planning on the part of the accused. In his case it was the similarities in the Bath and Farley Hill murders, to include the facts that these were all young girls, killed by manual strangulation without sexual interference, and without a struggle or attempt to hide the bodies.

In the opinion of the court, said Mr Justice Slade, this evidence was rightly admitted, not to show that Straffen was a professional strangler, but that he strangled Linda Bowyer.

The judge looked either side of him to see whether his colleagues wanted to add anything, but they shook their heads.

'In the circumstances this appeal is dismissed,' he announced and, after refusing leave to appeal further to the House of Lords, the three judges rose to their feet, gave the court a short bow and left.

This left John Straffen with fifteen days before he was due to be executed at Wandsworth Prison.

35

On the morning of Friday 29 August 1952, nine days after the appeal and a week before the execution date, John Straffen was lying on his bunk in the condemned suite in Wandsworth Prison, a position he'd maintained for most of the time during his stay in the condemned suite. He hadn't talked much except to ask when he wanted something. He'd been interested to read about himself in the papers, but there hadn't been much since the appeal. He didn't read the weeklies, but much of the comment had come from the weekly magazines.

For example, the edition of *Medical World* that week cynically thought it said much for the educative system at Broadmoor that it was able to turn Straffen from being unfit to plead on the first two murders into one who knew the nature and quality of his act and that he was doing wrong. It said little for the sanity of the law that the same man, who had been certified twice as mentally defective, whose mental age was about 9, and whose electroencephalograms indicated wide and severe damage in the cerebral cortex, probably from an attack of encephalitis in India before the age of 6, was found without legal guilt and confined to the 'safe custody' of Broadmoor for the first two killings, and found guilty of murder and sentenced to the extreme penalty of the law for the same crime only six months later.

'It is only because we know the more obvious fatuities of the law are generally corrected by the Home Secretaries that this sort of thing is tolerated,' the article concluded.

The Economist was less critical, saying there was no doubt of Straffen's earlier unfitness to plead, but that his six-month stay in Broadmoor had adjusted him sufficiently to appreciate, however dimly, what was happening in the recent trial: 'What could not have been altered was his mental deformity; Straffen was, and is, a certified mental defective.'

But the public mood was changing towards the death penalty. The horrors and bloodshed of a world war were still fresh in the public mind without having to add deaths by execution. A poll in the *Daily Mirror* showed that 65 per cent of readers wanted to reprieve John Straffen. A letter had come in to the paper from a London reader saying her child had been murdered three years ago, but that the murderer had been reprieved and sent to Broadmoor. Despite her earlier satisfaction at his appeal failing, 'I no longer have the shadow of the gallows hanging over the memory of my beloved baby,' she wrote. 'Surely it is the duty of every citizen to ensure that such individuals are given a chance to regain their health and self-esteem. Can we put an onus on such a man as Straffen because the authorities in charge of him failed to take the precautions that he remained in Broadmoor? To the mothers of the three children I would say: I know your sorrow and bitterness. I have been through it myself. But think deep down in your hearts. The satisfaction of knowing that your children's murderer had paid the supreme penalty will not give you the peace of mind you are looking for. Only God in His good time will give that, and when that comes you will thank Him for having given you the courage to put your Christian principles before all else.'

The Revd Eric Rees wrote from North London that Straffen was as much to be pitied as his own unfortunate victims. If our officially Christian state were to execute Straffen, he wrote, on the basis of the fundamentally barbarian and anti-Christian principle of retribution, every one of us would be involved in a ghastly sin.

John Straffen should have been relieved that the prison chaplain was not accompanying the Wandsworth Prison Governor when he suddenly turned up in the condemned suite that Friday morning. Even then John was not convinced this wasn't the execution party bringing the date forward a week.

The governor was clutching a piece of paper, which John thought might be his death warrant, like they brought to prisoners in the Tower when they did it in history at school.

'Well, Straffen,' he said as if he were addressing a schoolboy, 'I have to tell you that the Home Secretary has granted you a reprieve.'

John was struggling with the idea of a reprieve. 'I thought it was going to be next Thursday,' he said.

The governor read out the formal contents of the letter, which meant even less to John. Seeing the difficulty Straffen was having, he added, 'This means that you won't be hanged, not next Thursday or any time.'

John, who'd been standing stiffly to attention, relaxed slightly and brought a hand up to his mouth. 'That's good news, then.'

The governor nodded, not only because he agreed with the first judge that hanging this prisoner would be like executing a baby in arms, but also because he found his having to attend executions the grimmest part of his role as prison governor. In fact the first person he'd told that morning when he received the letter was the chaplain, who shared his distaste for the whole business.

The news understandably did not go down so well with the families of the victims. Arthur Pullen, Brenda Goddard's foster-father, told the newspapers, 'All I can say is that I am completely disgusted. If Straffen is to go back to Broadmoor it looks as though all the protests and petitions by parents worried about the safety of their children have been in vain.'

Cicely Batstone's mother said, 'This is terrible. We do not want to be vindictive, but the lives of three little children have already been lost and I cannot help wondering whether that is the end of the story.'

Mr Pullen's fears of John Straffen being returned to Broadmoor were immediately allayed by the Home Office announcement that his sentence would become life imprisonment and that he would serve this in prison and not Broadmoor – which in turn meant that with full remission he could be released after twelve or fifteen years.

The unanswered question on most minds was, if John Straffen had been reprieved because the Home Secretary had decided he was insane after all, why wasn't he being returned to Broadmoor for proper treatment as a patient rather than a prisoner, however inadequate the security at Broadmoor – or, if Straffen was sane, then why wasn't he being executed for the murders of three innocent children?

PRIME MINISTER'S
PERSONAL MINUTE

6

SERIAL No. M 471/52.

<u>HOME SECRETARY.</u>

I am somewhat concerned at the present position about Straffen. He was reprieved because he was a lunatic. Now he is to serve a life sentence as a criminal, which means that he may be released after fifteen years. It is difficult to see the logic of this. I should have thought that, in view of the decision which you took to reprieve him as a lunatic, he should go to the asylum and be detained at the Royal Pleasure. The fact that you do not send him there may be taken as an admission that security conditions do not prevail at Broadmoor. If there are proper security conditions, what is the reason for treating a lunatic, whom you have reprieved, as if he were a convict criminal?

We must I think discuss this matter in Cabinet before Parliament meets.

W.S.C.

5.9.52.

Churchill's Minute 5 September 1952. *The National Archives*

36

This was also the question being asked by the Prime Minister on the day originally fixed for the execution. On 5 September 1952 Winston Churchill wrote to his Home Secretary, Sir David Maxwell Fyfe, in a memorandum that has now been released into the public domain:

> I am somewhat concerned at the present position about Straffen. He was reprieved because he was a lunatic. Now he is to serve a life sentence as a criminal, which means that he may be released in fifteen years. It is difficult to see the logic of this. I should have thought that, in view of the decision which you took to reprieve him as a lunatic, he should go to the asylum and be detained at the Royal Pleasure. The fact that you do not send him there may be taken as an admission that security conditions do not prevail at Broadmoor. If there are proper security conditions, what is the reason for treating a lunatic, whom you have reprieved, as if he were a convict criminal?
>
> We must I think discuss this matter in Cabinet before Parliament meets.

Churchill was apparently as much in the dark as the rest of the nation as to why Straffen had been reprieved. When granting a reprieve Home Secretaries traditionally did not give their reasons, but it is surprising that the reprieve had not been discussed in Cabinet when the escape and the security issue at Broadmoor had been discussed both in Cabinet and in Parliament.

Prime Minister.

I have received your minute of 5th September (M.471/52).

Straffen was reprieved, not as a lunatic, but because he was sufficiently mentally defective not to be fully responsible for his crimes.

When a murderer is reprieved on the ground of mental defect he is normally sent by order of the Home Secretary to the Rampton State Institution for Mental Defectives from which he cannot be discharged without the consent of the Home Secretary and from which he would not be discharged unless the Home Secretary were satisfied that this could be done safely. There is no question of considering the release of a mental defective merely because he has been detained for so many years.

In view of the apprehension about Straffen, I decided that in the first instance he should be detained in a prison which the public accepted as secure and that the question of his transfer should be postponed for the present. But this does not in any way imply that I think that he should be considered for discharge after a certain number of years. Indeed, as I

/told

Home Secretary's Reply to Churchill, page 1 of 2, 8 September 1952. *The National Archives*

The Home Secretary replied to his Prime Minister three days later on 8 September as follows:

> Straffen was reprieved, not as a lunatic, but because he was sufficiently mentally defective not to be fully responsible for his crimes.
>
> When a murderer is reprieved on the grounds of mental defect he is normally sent by order of the Home Secretary to the Rampton State Institution for Mental Defectives from which he cannot be discharged without the consent of the Home Secretary and from which he could not be discharged unless the Home Secretary were satisfied that this could be done safely. There is no question of considering the release of a mental defective merely because he has been detained for so many years.
>
> In view of the apprehension about Straffen, I decided that in the first instance he should be detained in a prison which the public accepted as secure and that the question of his transfer should be postponed for the present. But this does not in any way imply that I think he should be considered for discharge after a certain number of years. Indeed, as I told the Cabinet on 4 September, I have recorded on Straffen's file the opinion that unless there is a marked change in his mental state, he should not be released at all.

While Churchill was as usual asking questions that went to the heart of the matter, he was using questionable language in doing so. Dr Hopgood, who'd resigned after twenty-seven years as Broadmoor's progressive and enlightened superintendent, would have despaired to hear his Prime Minister describe one of his patients as a lunatic, and his hospital as an asylum. In fact John Straffen had never been certified as insane throughout these various proceedings: at Taunton he was found unfit to plead, albeit on the evidence of one doctor, and after escaping from Broadmoor he was found by five doctors as fit to stand trial and sane. This was a point made by the trial judge at the second trial, and while it was harsh of *Medical World* to talk about the sanity and fatuities of the law, the fact remained that the law of murder needed changing to cover cases like this.

Five years after his conviction for the murder of Linda Bowyer, Parliament passed the Homicide Act in 1957 introducing the defence of diminished responsibility to murder, reducing it to manslaughter. This addressed the problems raised by cases like those of John Straffen, mental defectives in the old language, suffering from arrested or retarded development. No longer did a defendant have to show he or she was insane to escape the gallows.

Despite being the person he was, a man of low intelligence and timid by nature, most of the time saying very little unless it was to ask for something, John Straffen continued to be regarded as an escape risk by the Home Office. In 1956 he was moved to Horfield Prison, Bristol, after an escape attempt was discovered at Wandsworth by prisoners who intended to take John with them as a diversion, although liability might have been a better description. The move caused so much concern in Bristol, with a petition signed by 12,000 people demanding he be moved elsewhere, that he was transferred to Cardiff Prison. Then in 1966 a new high security wing was completed at Parkhurst Prison on the Isle of Wight and Straffen was the first to be moved into the wing, ahead even of the Krays and six of the Great Train Robbers.

Then in 1968 he was moved to Durham Prison and placed in the top security E wing where he was joined by Ian Brady. He was still there in 1984 when he became the country's longest-serving prisoner.

No Home Secretary agreed to release John Straffen, and in 1994 Michael Howard made up a list of twenty prisoners who would never be released, with John in the list.

The only other punctuation point to relieve the monotony of prison life came with an application in 2002 to the Criminal Cases Review Commission. John made the application himself for his case to be reviewed, and he was then represented by solicitors. However the CCRC turned down the application after considering the issues of prejudicial publicity at the time of the trial and whether the conviction for Linda Bowyer was safe.

In 2006 a fellow prison inmate described John as still lively, working as a cleaner in the craft shop and making tea for the officers. Apparently other prisoners left him alone and he was instantly recognisable, which probably wasn't surprising as his head was now shaven, emphasising the size of his head after encephalitis.

John Straffen died in the medical wing of Frankland Prison, County Durham on 19 November 2007, by which time he'd spent fifty-five years in prison. He never admitted to the murder of Linda Bowyer and had told his solicitor that he felt terrible about the first two murders, and wanted to be released from prison to live somewhere quiet.

BIBLIOGRAPHY

Adamson, Iain, *A Man of Quality – A Biography of Mr Justice Cassels* (London: Frederick Muller, 1964).

Baron-Cohen, Simon, *Zero Degrees of Empathy* (Allen Lane, 2011).

Fairfield, Letitia and Fullbrook, Eric (ed.) *The Trial of John Thomas Straffen* (William Hodge, 1954).

Hodge, James H. (ed.), *Famous Trials 8* (London: Penguin Books, 1963).

Partridge, Ralph, *Broadmoor* (London: Chatto & Windus, 1953).

Real-Life Crimes (London: Eaglemass Publications, 1994).

INDEX